## ACKNOWLEDGEMENTS

My special thanks must go to Brian Leng who first persuaded me I had a story to tell and who has helped me enormously during the writing of this book. I am also indebted to Paul Briggs of twocan design for his excellent graphic design skills and also his tireless work to ensure the publication came to fruition.

I would also like to thank my former managers Len Ashurst, Steve Fleet and Lawrie McMenemy and my Radio Newcastle co-commentator Nick Barnes for their contributions to the book and also Sunderland AFC publications editor Rob Mason for his advice and guidance throughout the project.

## a twocan publication

ISBN 978-0-9566798-3-3

**PICTURES:** Action Images, Paul Days, Bob Dixon, Terry Downey, Mirrorpics, North East Press, North News, The Northern Echo, Press Association, Rufus Abajas, Scarborough Evening News, Show Racism the Red Card & Sunderland AFC.

# the Black Cat

# Gary Bennett's football scrapbook

### Gary Bennett with Brian Leng

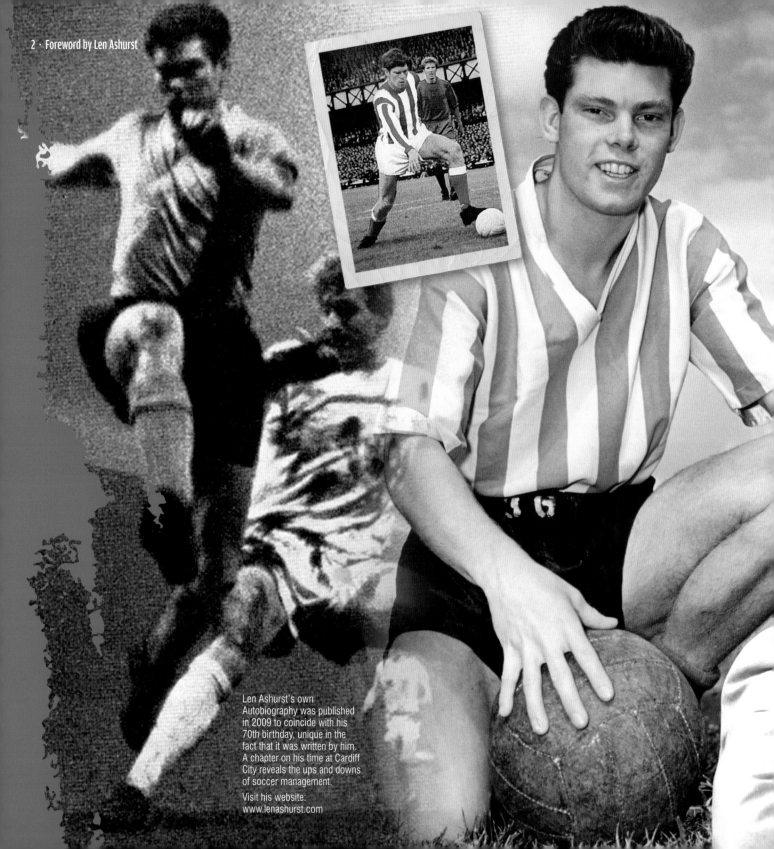

2 · Foreword by Len Ashurst

Len Ashurst's own Autobiography was published in 2009 to coincide with his 70th birthday, unique in the fact that it was written by him. A chapter on his time at Cardiff City reveals the ups and downs of soccer management.

Visit his website: www.lenashurst.com

as he relates to his family, friends and his many supporters the twists and turns of his football career and his success as a summariser on BBC Radio Newcastle, also a figurehead since it's inception in 1995 in his campaigning for his charity 'Show Racism the Red Card.'

I was very fortunate when joining Cardiff City as their manager in March 1983 in having two extremely talented young black footballers in the dressing room, yes the other one being Gary's brother David. They both went on to have very successful professional football careers and certainly in the time that I was manager at Cardiff, they were in general the first names I would write on the team sheet. However at that time they did not come without a certain amount of baggage. Being young, talented and good looking they where at times in the 'Scatterbrain' category and it was often the case that I would have a call from a local pub or night club owner to tell me that they had attracted the interest of the locals on the Saturday night after a game, however I rarely acted upon this information as supporters everywhere like to 'gossip.' In addition as far as I was concerned police were never involved, they both performed on match days and as a 'Gaffer' that is all you ask.

As manager of Gary at that time I was really excited about having a player of such natural ability in my dressing room. There was very little I could teach him on the training ground, my main task was to harness this talent to maturity, this was time consuming, as I knew that at any time he could slip back in to the wrong company, as he originated from the toughest area of Manchester and knowing that quite often after a game, he would make his way home to his roots to see his parents and his pals from Moss Side!

I would hold my breath at times as I arrived at the club on a Monday morning hoping that there had not been a call bringing me bad news from the north west of England. Pleasingly maturity came very quickly and along with Phil Dwyer he was rock solid throughout season 1982·83 as Cardiff City won promotion from the old Third Division.

As a free transfer at that time he was a gift from the footballing gods and he went on to prove to his home town club that they had dropped a clanger in giving him a free transfer. Their loss was my gain as he was the first player on my wish list as I took over the reins at First Division Sunderland in March 1984. His transfer fee of around £70,000 was settled at a tribunal in Sheffield and he immediately made a huge footballing impact on Wearside. At that time I signed another black player in Howard Gale, Gary always maintained that it was a signing to keep him company, after all Sunderland and the North East in general had not been over imbued with black players and Gary was only the second in the club's history.

**He made a dream debut; any doubters amongst the fans were put to bed as he had a game to remember. For those supporters in amongst the 18,000 plus crowd on Gary's debut on Saturday, August 25th 1984, they will never forget his debut goal in the opening minutes against Southampton when he became an immediate local hero and was accepted as one of their own.**

I do have one regret, at that time I should have also signed his brother David who went on to play for Coventry City, he was a fine talent!

Gary can be proud of what he has achieved, originating from Moss Side in Manchester where sadly drugs and violence were part of the culture, he has risen above the crowd and as a mature adult has carved himself a career both in football and society in general. Well done Gary, I am proud to have been associated with you and to have had a certain influence in your life.

**Len Ashurst**

**From my earliest memories right up to the present day, football has always been an integral part of my life and this book is essentially a scrapbook of a career that still gives me enormous pleasure.**

The book has been written in collaboration with my good friends Brian Leng and Paul Briggs and is a product of the countless hours we spent together sorting though literally hundreds of images before arriving at the final selection. I have to say I enjoyed every minute of the process as numerous memories both good and bad were rekindled.

Life for me began in the terraced streets of Longsight, a predominantly black community on the outskirts of Manchester where Mam and Dad had set up home having left their homeland of Jamaica in search of a better life. Their dream was to own their own home, a goal they eventually achieved through sheer hard work and sacrifice - it was only a relatively modest semi-detached house but to them it was like owning Buckingham Palace!

I was one of six children in the Bennett household - my sister Sybil, step-sister Pat and brothers, Frankie, Wesley and Dave, which generally meant there was never a dull moment when we were all at home! From our earliest days, it was pretty clear that Dave and I both had something of a gift when it came to football although as youngsters we were more than happy simply kicking the ball around with our mates at every available opportunity.

**Like most kids we supported our local team, in our case Manchester City, never for a moment imagining that one day we would both be pulling on that famous light blue jersey. Dave was the first to join City, signing in August 1978 and I joined him there a year later to begin a career in professional football that would last over twenty years and a one that indirectly, still provides me with a living to this day.**

It has certainly been one hell of a ride and along the way I've had the good fortune to meet some wonderful people from within the game, many of whom have helped me enormously during my career.

## Most of all though, I couldn't have achieved any of this without the support of my lovely wife Audrey who I married in 1991 - the best move I ever made!

**Family portrait:** That's me on the left with Dad, Mam and brother Dave

Dave, Mam and I outside our home in Manchester

My brother Wesley

Dave and I in Sunday best

My brother Frankie

Sister Sybil

Mam and Dad on their wedding day

My Gran Ada

This is my Dad - notice the likeness!

These photographs show Clive Wilson and I attending a 'Walk with Riddim - Dance with Dragon' night at Moss Side Youth Club. In the picture at the top, Clive and I are sitting alongside the giant figure of legendary West Indian cricketer Clive Lloyd who lived in the Manchester area and had come along to lend his support to the event.

**The guy in the other photo is Billy Hughes MBE, a man who helped me enormously during my younger days. Billy pretty much dedicated his life to running the youth club, working tirelessly to help keep kids off the street and out of trouble and had it not been for his guidance and support during my early teens, goodness knows where I might have ended up!**

Whilst I didn't actually live in Moss Side, we did have family living there and I tended to spend most of my spare time in the area, particularly at the youth club which had various events arranged almost every night of the week.

**It was a close knit community in every sense with outsiders left in no doubt that they simply weren't welcome - if anyone inadvertently drove into the area, they needed to pray that the traffic lights stayed on green to allow a hasty departure!**

Burnage High School team 1975 - not too difficult to pick me out of this line up!

Moss Side Youth Club FC 1977. What a difference two years make, not sure about my hat though!

Gary was one of the boys who came to Manchester City during the late 1970s via the local soccer scene - Alex Williams, Clive Wilson and Gary's brother Dave were the others. They were all by then in the 17 years of age group and I could not believe my luck at being provided with such an array of talent at that late age!

Gary himself ticked all the right boxes: A very likable personality, a tall athletic build, great feet and heading ability together with a sound temperament and attitude. Manchester City during this period had an outstanding youth squad and were destined to appear in two consecutive FA Youth Cup finals. At that time I predicted that Gary together with Tommy Caton would provide City with a defensive backbone for many years to come.

Unfortunately a new manager, John Bond came into the club at that time with his own ideas and both Gary and his brother Dave soon found themselves playing their football in Wales for Cardiff City.

The Welsh club however provided them with the very platform they needed and they both went on to have great careers in the game at Sunderland and Coventry City respectively, becoming legends in their own right and making me a very proud man in the process.

*Steve Fleet*
*Youth Manager at Manchester City 1973-1981*

**MANCHESTER CITY YOUTH TEAM 1980**
Back l to r: Dave Fitzharris, Geoff Lomax, Gary Parkinson, Gary Bennett, Alex Williams, Tommy Caton, Ritchie Cunningham & Gareth Bees. Front Row l to r: Andy May, Steve Kinsey, Clive Wilson, Steve McKenzie, Andy Elliott, Gary Fitzgerald & Ross McGinn

## WELCOME CITY

We welcome tonight Manchester City in the second leg of the FA Youth Cup Final, and we kick off with the advantage of a 3-1 lead gained from the first leg last week.

Like ourselves the Maine Road club have a team of promising youngsters, one or two of whom have already had considerable first-team experience.

It is a particularly happy occasion for Aston Villa tonight in that during the last decade we have appeared in three Finals of the FA Youth Cup, yet this is the first one where the deciding leg has been held at Villa Park.

We won the Youth Cup for the first time at Liverpool in 1972 and we were beaten by Crystal Palace in a one-match Final which was played at Highbury, in 1978.

So tonight our supporters have the opportunity of being able to see a game on which the cup depends. It is particularly gratifying to us, because we have had excellent support from Villa fans for our endeavours in the Youth field over the past 10 years, not least because of the success we have had in producing our own players.

We hope, therefore, that tonight's clash will fit the occasion both in skill and substance and that, at the end, the fans will have had plenty to shout about.

## THE ROAD TO THE FINAL

### ASTON VILLA

ROUND 1   Bye
ROUND 2   v Derby County (H)
          3-2
          Birch, Heath, Walters
ROUND 3   v Hereford (A)
          5-0
          Taylor (2), Birch, Walters, Ames
ROUND 4   v Hartlepool (A)
          1-0
          Walters
ROUND 5   v WBA (A)
          1-1
          Walters
REPLAY    v WBA (H)
          3-2
          Walters, Jones, Own goal
SEMI-FINAL  v Millwall (A)
1st Leg     2-0
            Walters, Hopkins
SEMI-FINAL  v Millwall (H)
2nd Leg     0-0
            Aggregate score 2-0
FINAL       v Manchester City (A)
1st Leg     3-1
            Ames (3)

### MANCHESTER CITY

ROUND 1   Bye
ROUND 2   v Grimsby Town (A)
          1-0
          Bees
ROUND 3   v Lincoln City (H)
          4-2-0
          May, McGinn, Bees (2)
ROUND 4   v Sunderland (A)
          2-0
          Bees, May
ROUND 5   v Sheffield Wed. (A)
          1-1
          McGinn
REPLAY    v Sheffield Wed. (H)
          3-2
          McGinn, McKenzie, Parkinson
SEMI-FINAL  v Manchester Utd. (A)
1st Leg     0-0
SEMI-FINAL  v Manchester Utd. (H)
2nd Leg     3-1
            Kinsey, Wilson, McKenzie
FINAL       v Aston Villa (H)
            1-3
            McKenzie

**2nd Leg**
# ASTON VILLA
v
# MANCHESTER CITY

Wednesday
30th April
1980
Kick-off
7.00 p.m.

...'S PUBLICATION

5p

## TONIGHT'S LINE-UP

| ASTON VILLA (Claret and Blue) | | MANCHESTER CITY (Blue and White) |
|---|---|---|
| MARK KENDALL | 1 | ALEX WILLIAMS |
| ANDY TAYLOR | 2 | ANDY MAY |
| MARK JONES | 3 | RICHARD CUNNINGHAM |
| DAVID MAIL | 4 | GARY BENNETT |
| NOEL BLAKE | 5 | TOMMY CATON |
| MARK HUTCHINSON | 6 | ROSS McGINN |
| ROBERT HOPKINS | 7 | KEITH PARKINSON |
| PAUL BIRCH | 8 | STEVEN MACKENZIE |
| DUNCAN HEATH | 9 | GARETH BEES |
| TREVOR AMES | 10 | STEVE KINSEY |
| MARK WALTERS | 11 | CLIVE WILSON |
| | SUB | ANDY ELLIOTT |
| | | DAVID FITZHARRIS |

### OFFICIALS

REFEREE: MR. A GUNN, (SUSSEX)

LINESMEN:
MR. A. J. ELLIS (EXETER) — RED FLAG
MR. L. B. BEGAM (EXETER) — YELLOW FLAG

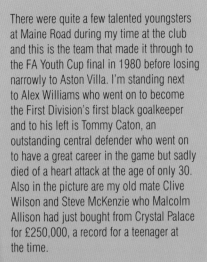

There were quite a few talented youngsters at Maine Road during my time at the club and this is the team that made it through to the FA Youth Cup final in 1980 before losing narrowly to Aston Villa. I'm standing next to Alex Williams who went on to become the First Division's first black goalkeeper and to his left is Tommy Caton, an outstanding central defender who went on to have a great career in the game but sadly died of a heart attack at the age of only 30. Also in the picture are my old mate Clive Wilson and Steve McKenzie who Malcolm Allison had just bought from Crystal Palace for £250,000, a record for a teenager at the time.

Quite a number of these lads went on to play in the City first team although unfortunately, I wasn't one of them. The arrival of John Bond signalled the end of my relatively short career at Maine Road and for a while it looked as though I might drift out of the game.

Then I received a phone call from former City stalwart Tony Book, who was coaching at Cardiff City, offering me the chance of a move to Ninian Park. I knew very little about the Welsh club other than the fact that they were in the Second Division, but I had no hesitation in signing as it was a great chance to resurrect my career and looking back, it was one of the best decisions I ever made!

I have to confess
that as an 18 year
old who'd lived in
Manchester all his life
and had never been
away from home,
the move down to Wales
did initially prove to be
a little daunting and I'll
never forget how nervous
I was travelling down
to Cardiff for my first game
at Ninian Park against
Welsh rivals Wrexham.

Best Wishes
Gary Bennett

The game was played on a Friday night and I came up against Dixie McNeil, a well-known striker and also a prolific goal-scorer in the lower leagues. However, much to the delight of our manager Ritchie Morgan, I had a particularly good game and kept the visitors' striker in check throughout although as soon as the final whistle blew I couldn't wait to get changed and head to the station for the next train back to Manchester.

**I jumped onto the first available train which unfortunately turned out to be the coal train which stopped at goodness knows how many stations before arriving at Crewe where I changed for Manchester, finally arriving home at six o'clock on Saturday morning!**

However, any chance of getting homesick was soon dispelled after only a few weeks when my brother Dave rang to let me know that Cardiff had offered Manchester City £100,000 for his services and the bid had been accepted by the City board. Whilst it was fantastic news for me personally, it was also something of a surprise as Dave was an established first-teamer at Maine Road who was more than capable of holding his own in the top flight and had played for City in the FA Cup final against Spurs just a few months earlier.

I had joined the massed ranks of City fans down to watch the final which ended in a 1-1 draw with City's Tommy Hutchison going into the record books as the first player to score for both teams in an FA Cup final. The replay the following Thursday turned out to be a classic with City leading 2-1 at one stage after a brilliant volley from Steve McKenzie had put them in front.

Then, after Garth Crooks netted an equaliser from close range, Ricky Villa produced one of the all-time great Wembley goals to win the game for Spurs. It was a truly amazing finish by the Argentinian international as he dribbled into the heart of the City box beating four or five defenders along the way before slotting the ball past big Joe Corrigan.

Having played at a club like Manchester City with so many star players in their ranks, the move to Cardiff did come as something of a culture shock for Dave and I, yet there's no question it proved to be the launching pad for both our careers. I've always maintained that my time at Ninian Park taught me a valuable lesson and it's a one which I've passed on to countless youngsters over the years. Whilst it's great to sign for a top club, the chances of breaking into the first team are invariably much less, particularly with the likes of Manchester City who, just as they are today, were massive spenders in the transfer market at the time, often preferring to use the cheque book to strengthen the team. Starting in the lower leagues gives young players a much greater chance of experiencing the rigours of first team football before attempting to move up to the higher level, assuming they're good enough of course!

**The turning point in my playing career came with the arrival of Len Ashurst as manager at Ninian Park although at the time I could hardly have imagined that this one man would change the path of my playing career in such a significant way. From day one I got on great with Len even though I apparently gave him a little bit of a worrying time each weekend when I returned home to Manchester to see my mates!**

Len had developed something of a reputation down in Wales having taken unfashionable Newport County into European football in the 1980-81 season when amazingly they reached the quarter finals of the Cup-Winners Cup and his arrival at Ninian Park in February 1982 was seen as a real boost for the club.

At the time, we were struggling in the lower reaches of Division Two and the directors had given Ritchie Morgan and his assistant Graham Williams their marching orders in the hope that a new manager would be able to save the club from the drop. Unfortunately, we fell just short finishing the season third from bottom, two points from safety. It was the following season when Len really began to have an impact at the club and we were never really out of contention in the promotion stakes finishing the campaign as runners-up to Portsmouth.

Cardiff City circa 1983

Trying to keep up with my brother Dave at Cardiff City's training ground,
now the site of the new Ninian Park

# 'Chucked out' — City star and ~~wife~~ Girlfriend

**SOCCER STAR** Gary Bennett and his wife were ordered out of a South Wales social club because the chairman "didn't like the look of them."

By Peter Bibby

The 21-year-old coloured Cardiff City defender was told to leave the Roath Carlylian Club in Splott — despite being signed in by a member.

The incident, on Sunday night, shocked other members of the club in Pearl Street and 24 hours later the chairman resigned after a furious row among the committee.

Gary and his wife Janet, who live in Dinas Powys, have now been sent an official apology and told they will be welcome at the club any time.

Within minutes of being signed into the club by freelance photographer Terry Downey, a member for 30 years, all three of them were ordered out by chairman Mr Freddie Osborne.

club and as chairman I could throw out who I liked. It had nothing to do with them being coloured. We've got coloured members and I'm not prejudiced."

The club secretary, Mr Kenny Payne, said: "Mr Osborne has been forced to resign from the committee and letters of apology are on the way to those concerned.

"This is a very unfortunate incident and Mr Osborne's views certainly do not reflect those of the committee. Mr Bennett and his wife and Mr Downey will be welcome here any time."

## 'No trouble'

"This was the first time this sort of thing had happened to me since I've been in Cardiff," said Gary. "It was very upsetting, especially for my wife.

"We were told we were not wanted and would have to leave immediately. We didn't want to argue about it so we all went."

After resigning from the club, Mr Osborne, of Zinc Street, Roath, said: "There was no trouble, I just chucked a couple of people out. That's all.

"I didn't know who they were and I didn't care. I didn't like the look of them and I wanted them out.

"It's a private social

This guy claimed he wasn't a racist - he just didn't like the look of the black couple who'd walked into his club!

Battling for possession with Dean Saunders in the local derby with arch rivals Swansea Ci

Entertaining local schoolchildren at Ninian Park

Hitting the net for Cardiff at Plymouth Argyle

Doing battle with Ipswich's Paul Mariner

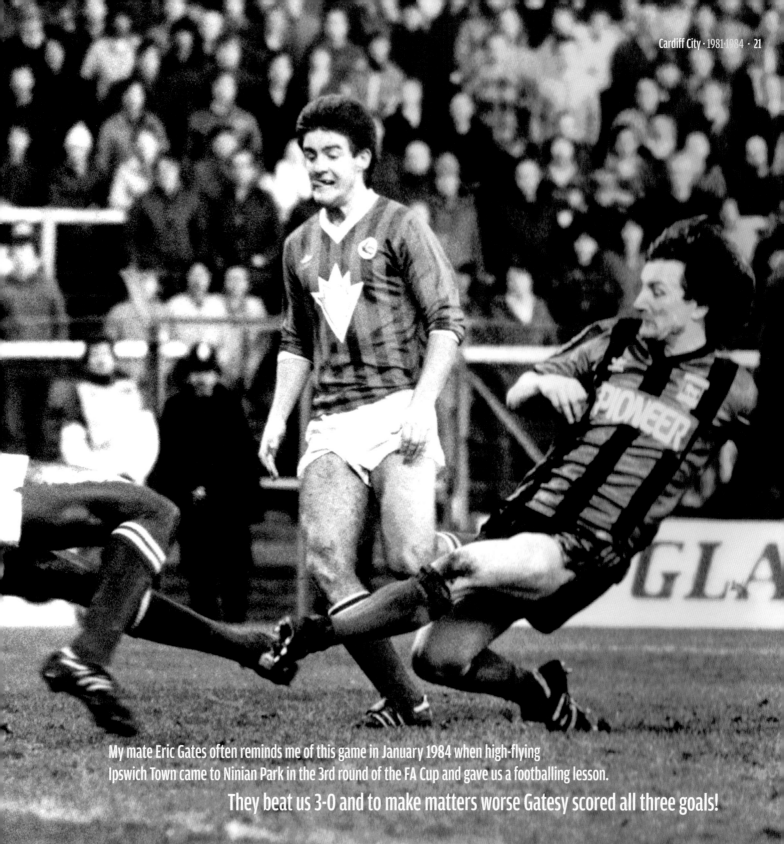

My mate Eric Gates often reminds me of this game in January 1984 when high-flying
Ipswich Town came to Ninian Park in the 3rd round of the FA Cup and gave us a footballing lesson.

They beat us 3-0 and to make matters worse Gatesy scored all three goals!

Professional football can be
a precarious occupation and often,
just when you're feeling really settled
at a particular club, events entirely beyond
your control can change the path of your
career almost overnight.

That was certainly the case
for me early in 1984 when,
completely out of the blue,
Len Ashurst announced that
he was leaving Ninian Park
to take over the vacant
manager's post at
Sunderland.

Things had been looking fairly positive at Ninian Park and Len was starting to mould the squad into quite a decent outfit.

In his first season he had led us back to the Second Division and with his sights now firmly set on promotion to the top flight, there was no indication that he might consider leaving the club. However, when Sunderland appeared on the scene the temptation was simply too great.

Not only were they a First Division outfit, it was also an opportunity for Len to fulfil a dream and return to manage the club where he had spent almost his entire playing career. During his 14 years at Roker Park he had become something of a legend on Wearside clocking up 452 appearances for the club, a record for an outfield player that still stands today.

When a manager leaves a club it can change things quite dramatically for the players he leaves behind who immediately begin to wonder who their next boss will be and whether they will figure in his plans. However, just before he left Ninian Park to take up his new appointment, Len called Andy Dibble and I into his office and reassured us of how highly he rated us as players and then said: 'Once I've settled in at Roker Park I'm hoping to come back here to sign you two, so make sure you stay close to the phone over the next couple of months!'

**Needless to say, the prospect of top flight football excited me greatly and in the weeks that followed I kept close watch on events at Roker Park where Len had inherited a talented but struggling team. His immediate priority was to stave off the threat of relegation, which he duly achieved although only a 2-0 victory over Leicester City on the final day of the season managed to ensure the club's First Division survival.**

The season over, I headed back home to Manchester and waited for the call that could launch me into the big time, however when the phone did ring it wasn't Sunderland but Crystal Palace chairman Ron Noades who was on the line telling me he was desperately keen to sign me.

To be honest, I wasn't sure how to react but, seeing as I hadn't heard anything from Len or Sunderland, I agreed to travel down to London to see what Palace had to offer.

I have to say I found Ron Noades to be a terrific guy and, as he and manager Steve Coppell outlined their plans for the club, their offer began to look very tempting. However, Len's promise and the prospect of the First Division were still niggling away at the back of my mind so I asked Palace if I could sleep on their offer and give them a decision the following day.

To be honest, my mind was in turmoil and I hardly slept a wink that night as I contemplated my future. The following morning Ron Noades was in touch first thing, in fact the phone hardly stopped as I discovered that the news of my possible move to Palace had leaked to the press, but I was still undecided. Then I picked the phone up for the umpteenth time to hear a gentleman with a north-east accent say: 'Hi Gary, my name's Barry Batey, I'm a director of Sunderland Football Club and we would like you to sign for us - you haven't signed for Palace have you?'

Barry explained that the maximum fee Sunderland could afford was £100,000 so as Cardiff City's valuation was higher than that, a tribunal would have to set the fee. The danger was that if the tribunal set the fee higher than £100,000 Sunderland would be forced to pull out and the whole deal would collapse.

Barry Batey

**My first taste of the Roker End!**

It was a risk, without doubt, but the prospect of playing in the top flight and teaming up with a manager who I rated so highly became the deciding factor.

In life you often reach a crossroads when a decision can take your future in a certain direction and had I signed for Palace that day my whole life would have changed completely. Apart from missing out on my playing career with Sunderland, I almost certainly wouldn't have met my wife and settled into a city that I love and now regard as my home. Also, I wouldn't be writing this book!

**The tribunal was arranged to meet at Sheffield United's Bramall Lane ground and as I drove across the Pennines that morning I couldn't help contemplating that when I travelled back later that day I might still be a Cardiff City player. In Sheffield I met up with Barry Batey and Len's number two, Frank Burrows and after an agonising wait, it was announced that the initial transfer fee had been set at £65,000 with further payments dependent on appearances. At last I was a Sunderland player!**

After the tribunal, I was ready to head back to Manchester but Barry insisted I travel up to Sunderland there and then. When I pointed out that I had no gear with me Frank Burrows piped up; 'Don't worry Gary, you're about my size so you can borrow some of mine.' Well, as nice a fellow as Frank is, I'm sure he won't mind me saying he's hardly the most fashionable guy in town, in fact anyone who has seen him standing on the touchline could be forgiven for thinking he's a farmer rather than a top flight football coach!

As we drove up through County Durham, Barry began pointing out all the mining villages that produced what he referred to as the 'hard core' of Sunderland's support. 'They're wonderful people Gary, and passionate about their team,' he said, 'hard working men who love their football and once a fortnight they converge on Roker Park in their thousands. Do the business for them and you'll be a hero for life!'

The one thing that had been concerning me about joining Sunderland was how the fans would react to a black player being in their team and as we pulled up outside of Roker Park I had my first indication that perhaps things might not go too smoothly.

New kids on the blocks - Steve Berry, yours truly, Clive Walker, Howard Gayle & Roger Wylde.

**Barry and I were heading towards the players entrance when a small group of youngsters approached us and asked: 'Who's this then Barry?' When Barry pointed out that I was Gary Bennett, the club's new signing from Cardiff City, one of the kids replied: 'But he's black!'**

A small incident maybe, but a clear indication that I might not be accepted by the Sunderland fans in quite the same way as I had been at Manchester and Cardiff. Contrary to the modern game, the general attitude towards black players in those days was appalling and, looking back, some of the abuse we had to endure was nothing short of disgusting. However, having grown up in a strong black community in Manchester, I was largely protected from any real problems of racial abuse and at both my previous clubs there had been a strong black presence in the dressing room. At Roker Park, it was different, I was on my own and on that very first day, I have to confess, feeling very exposed in a town that, as far as I could see, had very few black people.

Roger Wylde, Clive Walker and myself are happy to oblige as Len Ashurst shows off his new signings

Frank Burrows

It was something I discussed at length with Len Ashurst shortly afterwards and he pulled no punches telling me:

'Look Gary, if you perform as I know you can you'll have no problems with the fans. On the other hand, they love their football up here and at times they can be very critical. Like any other player, if you're not performing they'll be on your back and you'll be out of the door - it's a simple as that!'

**He then gave me some comfort by announcing that he was about to sign another black player, Howard Gayle from Birmingham City, saying: 'Howard will be a good mate for you!'**

In actual fact, Howard and I did become great pals and I suppose, in a way, helped each other through a potentially difficult period leading up to the first game of the new season. We weren't the only new arrivals at Roker Park that summer as Len set about rebuilding the team by signing the likes of Clive Walker, David Hodgson, Peter Daniel and Roger Wylde, however it was undoubtedly Howard and I that had the greater reason to feeling somewhat apprehensive as we ran out to face a packed Roker Park for the opening game of the season against Southampton.

**All I was hoping for was a steady performance to demonstrate to the Sunderland fans that their new signing from Cardiff City was a half-decent player, regardless of the colour of his skin. Even in my wildest dreams, I couldn't have imagined the events that were about to unfold in the first few minutes of the match.**

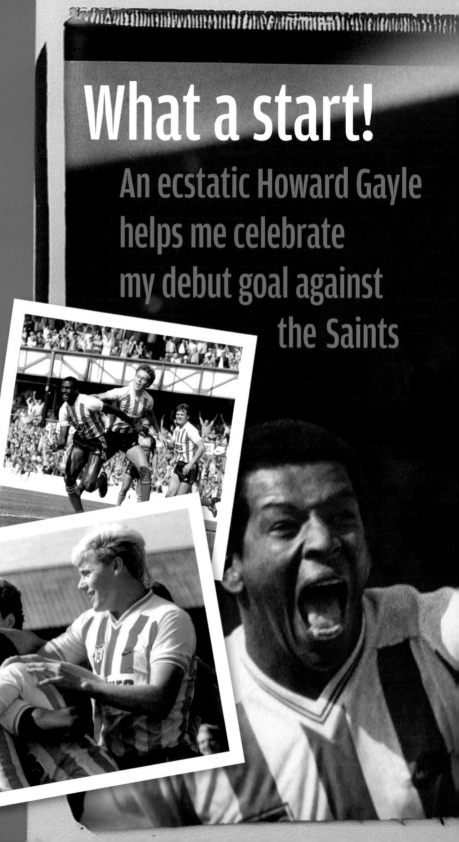

# What a start!

An ecstatic Howard Gayle helps me celebrate my debut goal against the Saints

Canon Official Programme. Canon League Division One Canon
**Sunderland v. Southampton**
Saturday, 25 August, 1984. Kick-off 3 p.m. - Programme 40p.

We were attacking the Roker End and I was up lending my weight to the attack when suddenly the ball was presented to me on the edge of the six-yard box. Instinctively, I fired in a first-time shot that flew past Peter Shilton in the Southampton goal and into the net to give us the lead. It was an incredible moment, real 'Roy of the Rovers' stuff, and it lifted the pressure immediately - from that moment on I could sense that the Sunderland fans were right behind me.

**We ended up winning the match 3-1 with Mark Proctor and Barry Venison netting our other goals giving us a fantastic start to the new campaign. It was a happy dressing-room that night with everyone full of optimism although none of us could have envisaged the roller coaster season that lay ahead.**

# Down but not out!

Fortunately I managed to recover fairly quickly from this injury and was able carry on and enjoy arguably our best performance in the league during the 1984-85 campaign.

Manchester United were the visitors to Roker and when they raced to a two-goal lead after only ten minutes it looked as though we were in for a real hiding.

However, in a truly amazing first half we managed to turn things around in the most dramatic fashion imaginable to lead 3-2 at the interval.

Clive Walker was the architect of United's destruction grabbing a hat-trick including two from the penalty spot.

On his day there were few more exciting players than Clive and that afternoon he ran the United defence ragged to secure a memorable victory.

**My first encounter with Newcastle United could hardly have been a more torrid affair and the abuse Howard Gayle and I had to endure from start to finish was something I had never experienced previously.**

# As a black player I'd taken my fair share of stick over the years but nothing quite like this.

Our confidence was raised a little during the warm-up when we noticed that one of the linesmen was Uriah Rennie, one of the few black officials in the game, however as the game progressed we soon realised that we would be getting no favours from the men in black!

The real controversy kicked off just after half-time when Wes Saunders went down in the box under a challenge from Howard Gayle and the referee immediately pointed to the spot. It was a nothing challenge and Saunders had gone down far too easily as far as we were concerned.

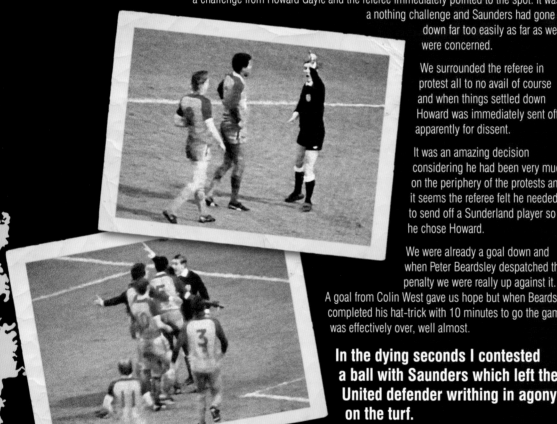

We surrounded the referee in protest all to no avail of course and when things settled down Howard was immediately sent off, apparently for dissent.

It was an amazing decision considering he had been very much on the periphery of the protests and it seems the referee felt he needed to send off a Sunderland player so he chose Howard.

We were already a goal down and when Peter Beardsley despatched the penalty we were really up against it. A goal from Colin West gave us hope but when Beardsley completed his hat-trick with 10 minutes to go the game was effectively over, well almost.

**In the dying seconds I contested a ball with Saunders which left the United defender writhing in agony on the turf.**

# Although I protested my innocence...

I found myself making the long walk off the park to a torrent
of abuse from the home fans and down the tunnel for an early bath,
not quite the finale I was hoping for in my first ever North-East derby!

# The Milk Cup

No one can say we were given an easy run on our way to the 1985 Milk Cup final and whilst our victory over Crystal Palace in Round 2 raised few eyebrows, the games that followed produced some unforgettable moments.

**Next up were Brian Clough's Nottingham Forest and a 1-1 draw at the City Ground set up an intriguing replay at Roker Park which was settled by a classic Howard Gayle strike in extra-time. It was a terrific moment as his shot from the edge of the box flew into the bottom corner of the net and he raced away in celebration with the crowd going crazy!**

A home tie against Tottenham Hotspur was our reward and the Londoners looked favourites to progress to the next round after a goal-less draw at Roker.

However, in the game at White Hart Lane we produced what I consider to be our best performance of the cup-run with goals from Clive Walker and Gordon Chisholm securing a great 2-1 victory although Chris Turner was our hero that night, making a string of wonderful saves including a Graham Roberts penalty late in the game.

Watford away is always something of a battle and our fifth Round tie proved to be no exception. I was out injured for this game and watched from the Vicarage Road terraces as Clive Walker netted the only goal of the game to settle the issue.

David Hodgson in action during the 3rd round tie with Nottingham Forest at the City Ground

Clive Walker takes on the Spurs defence during the 0-0 draw at Roker Park

# Watford 0 Sunderland 1...

## We were in the semi-final and about to face Chelsea in two games that would be talked about for years...

Chris Turner in the thick of the action at Vicarage Road during our 1-0 victory over Watford in the 5th round

# Healing hands...

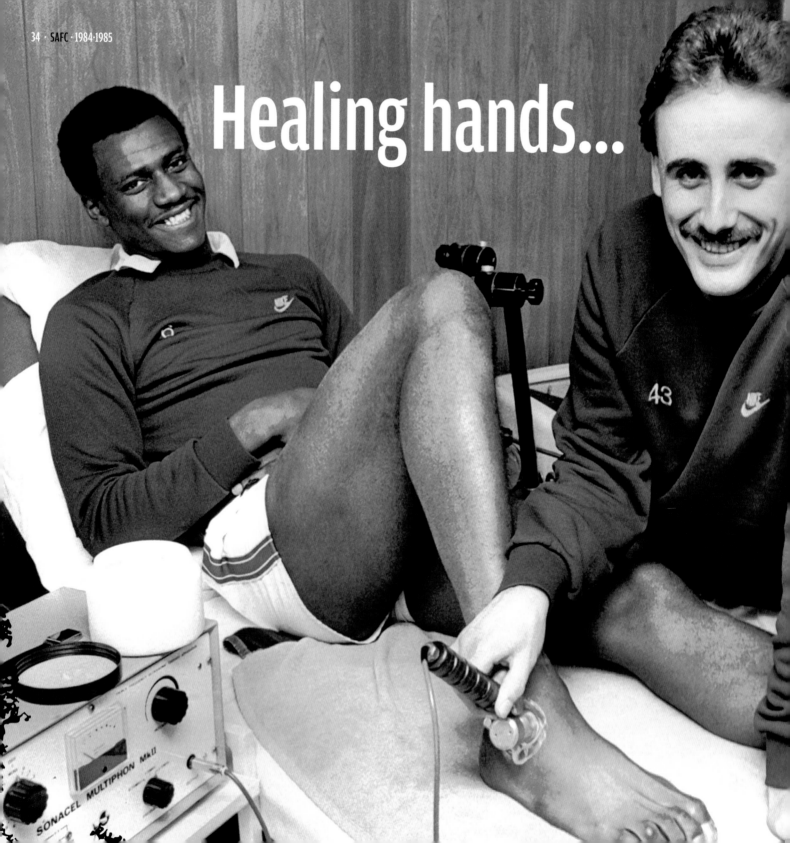

Physio Steve Mason makes sure I'm going to be fit for the forthcoming semi-final against Chelsea, although the equipment he's using does look a little dated compared to present day technology!

**Mind you, when I first started in the game the infamous 'Magic Sponge' was still very much the treatment for just about any injury incurred during a game. For the younger generation, this was nothing more than a common or garden sponge used to apply lashings of ice cold water to the area in question, which wasn't particularly pleasant if you'd suffered a groin injury!**

I'm not sure how the superstars of the modern game would react to this primitive and often painful treatment, but it didn't seem to do the players of our generation any harm and they certainly missed fewer matches through injury, that's for sure. When you consider the level of medical care that's available today you have to wonder why players spend so much time on the treatment table, or maybe the 'Magic Sponge' did have hidden powers after all!

Howard Gayle on the receiving end of the magic sponge treatment

# and the magic sponge!

# The Milk Cup
## semi-final 1st leg
## Sunderland 2
## Chelsea 0

Despite a desperate lunge,
I can't prevent Chelsea's Mickey Thomas
getting in his shot on goal.

The Milk Cup semi-final 1st leg against Chelsea at Roker Park produced a solid performance and a 2-0 victory that set us in good stead for the second leg at Stamford Bridge.

## It also produced my first confrontation with David Speedie or to be more precise, his father!

Speedie didn't play in the Roker match but he'd brought his father along to watch and after the game, in the players' lounge, he started having a go at the Sunderland players telling us exactly how his son was going to sort us out in the second leg.

He'd obviously had a drink or two and at first we tried to ignore him but on and on he went, ranting and raving about how good a player David was until eventually I told him to F.Off! After that things tended to get a bit nasty and that more or less set the mood for the second leg...

Clive Walker has just netted his second goal and Colin West and Steve Berry join in the celebrations

The second leg at Stamford Bridge certainly proved eventful for David Speedie, but not quite as his father had predicted. Even though he did give them an early lead, the game turned dramatically our way with Clive Walker returning to his old stamping ground to haunt the home side by scoring two goals and generally giving their defence a torrid time.

**Colin West added a third to secure a memorable 3-2 victory, with the icing on the cake coming a few minutes from time when Speedie was given his marching orders!**

Chelsea fans
on the rampage
after
Clive Walker's
second goal

# The Milk Cup
## Semi-final 2nd leg
## Chelsea 2
## Sunderland 3

These ugly scenes continued until the end of the game and there was even the amazing sight of a policeman chasing a Chelsea fan across the goalmouth as Colin West netted our third goal!
It was an atmosphere of pure hatred and it certainly wasn't confined to the terraces with our friend Speedie, not surprisingly, in thick of it.
Again, it all kicked off in the players lounge with poor Clive Walker the target and only the intervention of Mickey Droy, Chelsea's giant defender, prevented the incident turning to blows.

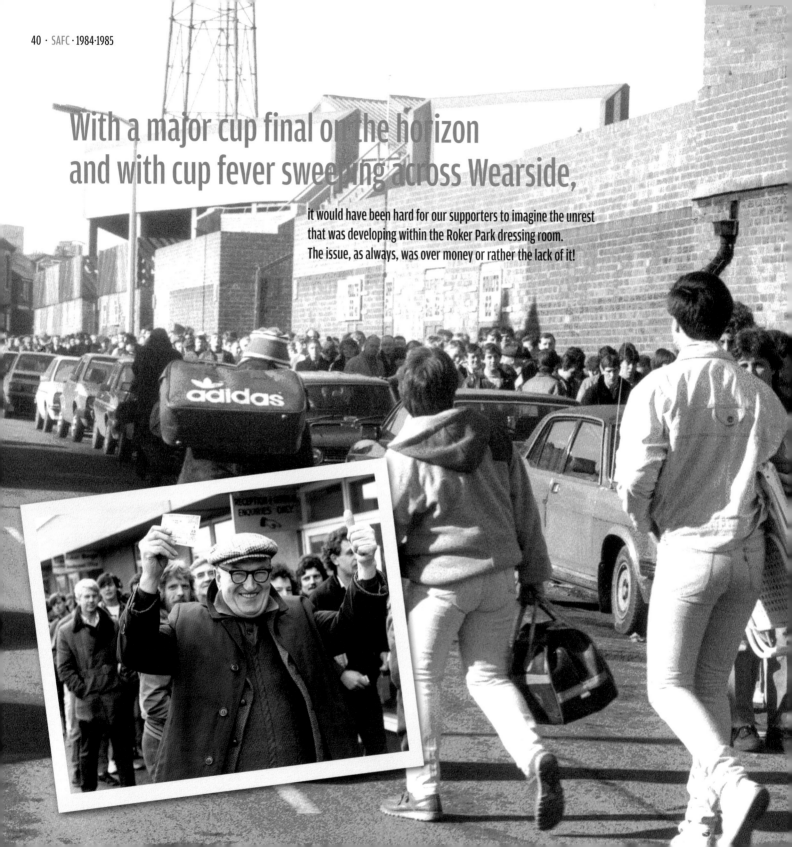

# With a major cup final on the horizon and with cup fever sweeping across Wearside,

it would have been hard for our supporters to imagine the unrest that was developing within the Roker Park dressing room. The issue, as always, was over money or rather the lack of it!

Some weeks previously, as our run in the Milk Cup was gathering momentum, the first team squad had been promised significant bonuses if we managed to make it through to the final. Now suddenly we discovered that the directors were denying any knowledge of such an agreement.

**Barry Batey, our main point of contact in the boardroom, had promised that the club would pay us £10,000 if we made it to Wembley and whilst it subsequently transpired that Barry had done this without discussing it with his fellow directors, as far as the players were concerned the club were now reneging on a formal agreement. Not surprisingly, we were furious.**

Then there was the issue of allocation of match tickets for the final at Wembley. This was always a touchy subject among supporters in those days, but as far as the players were concerned, it offered a way of making a little bit of extra money. When the club announced we would only receive four tickets each, you can imagine the reaction of the players.

Without wanting to sound mercenary, reaching a major final was always seen as an opportunity for players to benefit financially and 1985 was no exception. The lads had formed a players' pool on the basis that everything we brought in would be collected and shared out after the final. Typical sources of potential income were sponsorship, media work and of course, match tickets. This was the era of the ticket tout, generally a London-based character who would acquire tickets from whatever source and then sell them on to supporters at inflated prices. This practice was outlawed years ago but back in the 1980s it was still quite prevalent and I'll be surprised if any player appearing in a cup final at that time didn't profit to some degree by selling on tickets to the touts.

There were various ticket touts operating at the time but the name of one man was synonymous with the profession, Stan Flashman. One of the lads had a contact who knew Stan so disposing of the tickets wouldn't have been a problem for us providing we managed to persuade the club to increase our allocation.

**Eventually, after much debate and argument, we were allowed to purchase additional tickets so we did manage to make a bit of extra cash however, the whole business had simply served to sour relations between players and directors even further.**

Shaun Elliott

The man I felt sorry for during this whole sorry episode was Len Ashurst. On the one hand he was trying desperately to keep up morale in the dressing-room leading up to the big game whilst at the same time having to appease his bosses upstairs in the boardroom. His job was made even harder when another argument developed, this time over kit sponsorship or more specifically, boots. At the time the club had a playing kit deal with Nike and whilst some of the squad did continue to wear Nike boots, others had agreed separate deals with manufacturers such as Adidas and Puma.

The problem was, the club were insisting that everyone wore Nike boots for the final which meant that certain players would be penalised financially if they complied. This argument rumbled on right up to the day of the final with Barry Venison, who'd been made captain in Shaun's absence, sitting in the Wembley dressing-room and refusing to change his Adidas boots. It even got to the point where Len threatened to leave him out of the team unless he agreed. Fortunately, a compromise was reached with Frank Burrows feverishly applying black paint to hide the white stripes on Barry's boots as kick-off time approached, a bizarre situation and hardly the ideal preparation for one the biggest games in the club's history!

**Leading up to the final, we had been fielding a fairly settled side but Shaun Elliott's booking at Stamford Bridge meant he would miss leading out the team at Wembley, a devastating blow for a local lad who had come through the ranks at Roker Park. It also left Len Ashurst with a selection problem and one that would subsequently haunt him for years.**

Colin West had been one of our star performers in the cup run scoring three times in the semi-final games against Chelsea, but on the morning of the match he received the dreaded phone call asking him to go to the manager's room. Len explained that he had decided to play a sweeper system, bringing in young David Corner at the back and playing Ian Wallace up front as a lone striker...

Colin West scoring from the spot in the Milk Cup semi-final 1st leg at Roker Park

## ...Colin was out and, needless to say, he was absolutely devastated!

The Westmorland Hotel in London, our headquarters for the Milk Cup final

On the ball with Norwich winger
Louie Donowa in hot pursuit

In football, the dividing line between success
and failure can often be the finest of margins
and that was certainly the case in the Milk Cup
final against Norwich City.

As a spectacle, the game was
a poor affair with the result being
determined by two major incidents
early in the second half...

I manage to win this aerial battle with Dave Watson
and Steve Bruce but my header sails over the bar

The first, only a minute after the interval, brought the only goal of the game although there was a huge element of luck in the way it was scored. There seemed to be little danger as David Corner was policing the ball out for a goal-kick near the corner flag, but John Deehan managed to win possession for City and when he played the ball in, Asa Hartford fired a shot goalwards. Gordon Chisholm attempted to block the shot but only succeeded in deflecting the ball past Chris Turner and into the net.

Almost immediately we had a great chance to get back into the game when Barry Venison was tackled in the box by Van Wyk and as the City defender fell he scooped the ball away with his hand. The referee had no hesitation in awarding a penalty and as Clive Walker stepped up to take the kick I was certain he would net the equaliser.

**His record from the spot was excellent including two against Manchester United earlier in the season but on this occasion luck deserted him as his shot clipped the outside of the post and the chance was gone.**

After that we rarely looked like scoring and at the final whistle came the harsh realisation that we had lost a massive game that was clearly within our capabilities of winning. It's impossible to describe the feeling of disappointment I experienced at that moment but I learnt one thing that day...

## Wembley is no place for losers!

Len Ashurst with Norwich boss Ken Brown

WEMBLEY STADIUM

The Milk Cup Final

SUN., 24 MARCH, 1985
KICK-OFF 2.30 p.m.

YOU ARE ADVISED TO TAKE UP YOUR POSITION BY 2.00 p.m.

TURNSTILES
D
ENTRANCE
8
EAST
LOWER
STANDING
ENCLOSURE

654

RESERVED
STANDING
PLACE
£5.00

TO BE RETAINED

ISSUED SUBJECT TO THE CONDITIONS ON BACK

Milk Cup Final

Norwich City
v
Sunderland

Sunday 24th March 1985 Kick-off 2·30

Wembley Stadium
OFFICIAL SOUVENIR PROGRAMME          80p

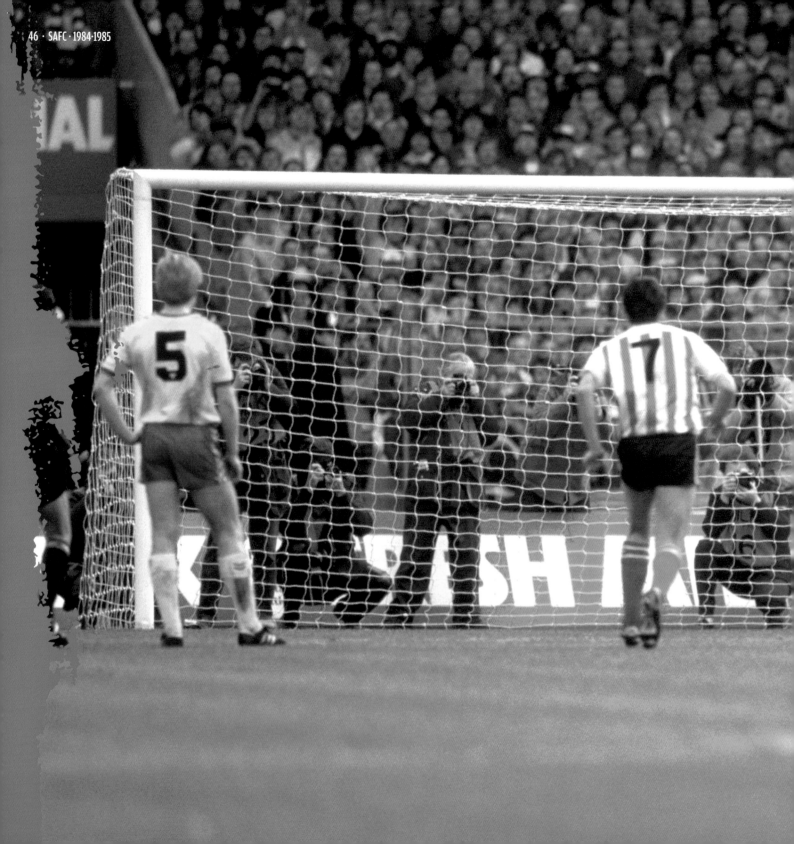

# So close....

Clive Walker's penalty strikes the outside of the post and the chance of an equaliser has gone.
This was undoubtedly the turning point of the game and desperately unfortunate for Clive
who had been superb for us during the cup run.

The final whistle has blown and Norwich City celebrate. There's no worse feeling than losing a Wembley final – our players were heartbroken and desperately disappointed for our supporters who had been absolutely magnificent throughout the cup run.

# Unfortunately, worse was to follow...

...bitter
disappointment

David Corner

A season which had promised so much was suddenly turning sour and after the devastating defeat at Wembley it was hardly surprising that our league form would suffer, although few could have envisaged that the campaign would end in relegation.

**Our fate was finally sealed following a 4-0 defeat at Aston Villa in our third from last game, although by then relegation was merely a formality. We had managed just one victory in the 12 games that followed the Milk Cup final finishing the season 10 points from safety and it came as no surprise when Len Ashurst was dismissed shortly afterwards.**

Len had taken the brunt of the criticism for the Wembley defeat with most supporters blaming his team selection, and particularly the omission of Colin West and the selection of David Corner, as the reason for our inability to overcome a fairly ordinary Norwich City side. Colin never forgave Len and I heard that years later when Len offered to give him his own Milk Cup Final medal in the way of compensation, Colin told him exactly where to stick it!

The general consensus among the squad was that Colin should have played in the final and speaking personally, I felt he would have given us the physical presence we needed up front against City's formidable central defenders Steve Bruce and Dave Watson. Having said that, we had beaten the Canaries 3-1 on their own patch without Colin eight days earlier and Ian Wallace had weighed in with one of the goals so perhaps you could see the logic in Len sticking with the same striking formation for the final.

Colin went on to carve out a decent career in the game but for David Corner the legacy of his Wembley mistake lived on even after he'd retired from the game. This was perhaps best illustrated some years later when David, having joined the police force, was responding to a report of two men fighting at a house in Seaham. When he arrived at the scene he found one man lying injured outside the property and the other, inside the house, semi-conscious and bleeding heavily from a head wound. As David administered first aid the guy gradually came around, stared at this blurred image of a policeman for a while and then said: 'Why didn't you kick it out for a corner!' For Sunderland fans, even in their worst moments of adversity, football always comes first!

For me personally, my first season at Roker Park had turned into a one of huge disappointment. Apart from events on the pitch, my partner Janet and I had found it terribly hard to settle on Wearside. Moving to a new town in a different part of the country is always a traumatic time but in those days it was doubly difficult for a black family to integrate into a new community, particularly one with so few black people.

At least I was able to head off to training each day whereas Janet felt completely isolated with no friends or family to rely on for support. The situation put a tremendous strain on our relationship and eventually she returned home to Manchester with our children Leon and Janee. At that moment it would have been impossible to imagine that I would go on to make well over 400 appearances for Sunderland and end up making my home on Wearside.

Colin West

# Enter
# Lawrie...

one of the biggest names
in English football at the time...

With Sunderland now back in Division 2 and morale among players and supporters alike at an all-time low, it was hard to imagine how any top manager would be attracted to the club yet incredibly, our chairman Tom Cowie was able to pull off a massive coup and persuade Southampton boss Lawrie McMenemy to move to Wearside and take over the vacant manager's chair at Roker Park.

Lawrie was one of the biggest names in English football at the time having taken unfashionable Southampton from Second Division obscurity to the higher echelons of the top flight as well as winning the FA Cup with a 1-0 victory over Manchester United at Wembley in 1976. At the Dell he had assembled an impressive squad and had managed to persuade top international players such as Kevin Keegan, Alan Ball and Peter Osgood to move to the south coast club. Lawrie had also established himself as a major figure in the media appearing regularly on television and was tipped by many to be the next England boss.

'I may not have enjoyed the best of times at Sunderland, but one decision I did get right was appointing Gary Bennett as team captain. At Southampton I had no fewer than six England captains at the club - Alan Ball, Mick Channon, Kevin Keegan, Mick Mills, Peter Shilton and Dave Watson - so I think I can rightly claim to being pretty well qualified when it comes to spotting the qualities necessary to make a good skipper!

To be honest, Gary was the obvious choice from the first time I saw him play and the fact that he was black never entered my head. Apart from his obvious skills as a player, I immediately saw that he commanded total respect from everyone around him and I soon established that he was also someone I could trust implicitly. Unlike many captains, Gary wasn't a 'shouter', but his colleagues were never left in any doubt as to who was in charge out on the park!

When I arrived at Sunderland, my plan was simply to try and repeat the success that I had enjoyed at Southampton where my philosophy had been to bring in quality performers to supplement the more workmanlike players in the squad, 'violinists and road-sweepers', as I used to call them. You would never win anything with a team made up entirely of 'violinists', you always needed a few 'road-sweepers' in there to carry out the less glamorous tasks - it was all about having the right balance. It worked wonderfully well for me at Southampton but the fact that I was unable to replicate the same sort of success at Roker Park still upsets me to this day. However, in my defence, there were hugely mitigating circumstances and one day I might be tempted to write a book and reveal exactly what went on behind the scenes during my two years at the club!

I was delighted, but not surprised that Gary went on to have such a great career at Sunderland, and the fact that he made almost 450 appearances for the club and still remains as popular as ever with Sunderland fans tells its own story - an excellent footballer and a smashing fella!'

Lawrie McMenemy

My initial impression of Lawrie was certainly positive as he explained to the players that having been born and brought up in the North East, he fully appreciated the passion of our supporters and also stressing that he shared their desire for success. Indeed, as our new boss quickly added the likes of Eric Gates, Alan Kennedy, George Burley and Dave Swindlehurst to our ranks, it was hard to imagine anything other than a quick return to the First Division.

'Lawrie meets the fans and outlines his plans for getting Sunderland out of the Second Division.

At the time few could have predicted how he would ultimately achieve that goal!'

There was something of a carnival atmosphere inside Roker Park when we ran out to face Blackburn Rovers for the opening game of the 1985-86 season with the biggest cheer undoubtedly reserved for our new manager as he made his way to the dug-out.

However, any hopes of a flying start to the season were soon put in check as a resolute Rovers side set about spoiling the party, scoring twice in the second half to secure all three points. Not exactly the flying start to the season we'd hoped for but much worse was to follow in the weeks that lay ahead.

**Successive defeats at Portsmouth and Crystal Palace followed by a 3-0 hammering at home to Oldham Athletic and a 1-0 reverse at Millwall certainly started the alarm bells ringing. The statistics made frightening reading...**

# played 5, lost 5, 10 goals conceded
## and, even worse, we hadn't managed to score a single goal!

Now rooted firmly at the bottom of the league, the chips were certainly down when we lined up against Grimsby Town for our third home game of the season.

Ian Wallace in the thick of the action

Shaun Elliott and I lend our weight to the attack in the opening game of the season against Blackburn Rovers

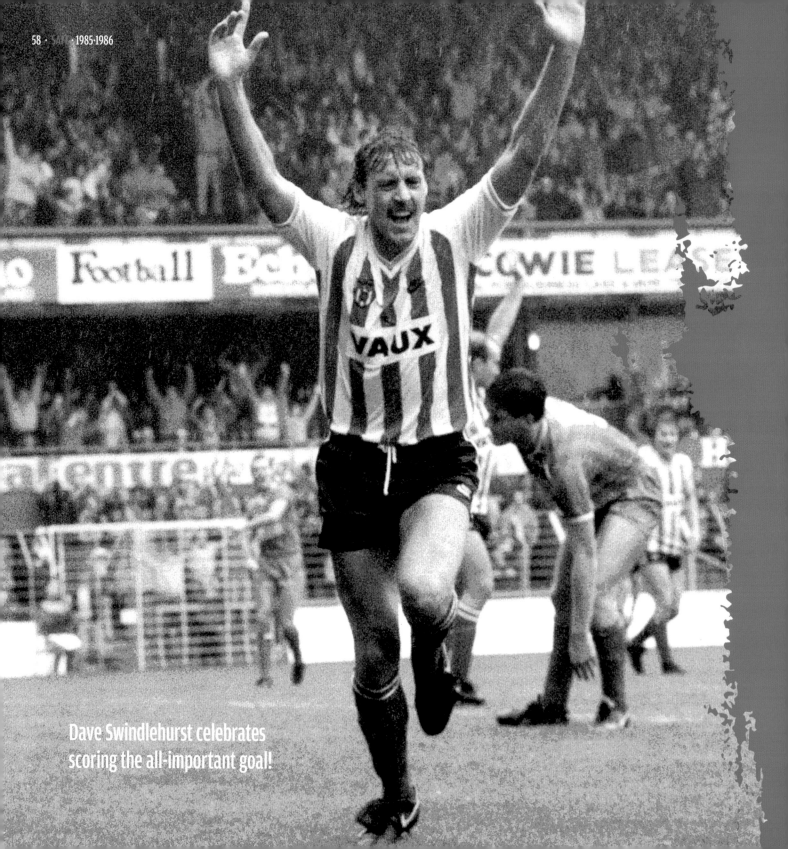

Dave Swindlehurst celebrates
scoring the all-important goal!

# ...a goal at last!

## After no less than 494 minutes of football, a club record for the start of a season, we finally managed to get off the mark!

Dave Swindlehurst was the man who claimed the dubious distinction of being the scorer of that first goal against Grimsby Town and even though we managed to add two more in the second half, they were only sufficient to earn a share of the spoils in a 3-3 draw.

**For a short while it looked as though the tide might have turned but it seemed that every winning performance would inevitably be followed by a defeat as we found it almost impossible to string a decent run of results together. The optimism of that opening day now seemed a million miles away as we faced up to the very real possibility of being drawn into a relegation battle.**

Quite why things were going so badly wrong was difficult to understand bearing in mind the quality of the players we had in the side. No one could dispute the fact that Lawrie had brought in some very good players, particularly the likes of Alan Kennedy, Eric Gates and George Burley all experienced internationals with glittering club careers behind them.

Personally, I felt one or two of our more talented players were struggling to come to terms with the rigours of Second Division football which in those days was much quicker and more physical than the top flight where the more cultured players were given the time and space to display their skills.

To be fair, I think Lawrie was as bemused and frustrated as anyone. At Southampton his senior players pretty much ran the show with regard to tactics and such like but when this didn't work for him at Sunderland, he seemed unable to produce the managerial guidance and motivation that could have helped us arrest the slide. Having started the season as odds-on promotion favourites, we now found ourselves going into the final game of the season against Stoke City at Roker Park needing a victory to avoid the ignominy of relegation into English football's third tier.

Alan Kennedy

Eric Gates

George Burley

Lawrie acknowledges the cheers of the fans after witnessing a 2-0 victory over Stoke City which ensured our Second Division survival at the end of his first season in the Roker Park hot seat.

**His 'surrender' gesture with the white handkerchief was his way of acknowledging the disappointments of a dreadful campaign and on the day the fans went home happy and relieved.**

Alan Kennedy takes on the Stoke defence

However, the unrest that had been gathering momentum among our supporters was fuelled even further when the club accounts were published during the close-season.

Apparently, Lawrie had been paid £166,000 in his first year in charge, a staggering amount in those days which made him far and away the highest paid manager in English football!

Ian Wallace, Tony Ford and Barry Venison leave the pitch after the 2-0 victory over Stoke City had guaranteed our survival

Tony Ford tries his luck with a shot on goal

COWIES
FORD SURE
MDON ST. TEL 40311.

WHAT ALL CAR
SERVICING
SHOULD BE LIKE

Smiling all the way to the bank.

# Lawrie's £166,000 a year

**ERLAND** managing director Lawrie ... paid a staggering £4,000 per week ... ... the Prime Minister — ... of a million pounds

We had seen very little of Lawrie out on the training pitch during that dreadful first season with Lew Chatterley and John Sainty pretty much running the day to day coaching of the first team.

Both had followed Lawrie from Southampton together with his son Chris who was given the task of looking after the youth team. When his second campaign in charge produced little or no improvement, Lawrie became more involved including, among other things, introducing us to 'shadow training'. Basically, this was a full-scale practice match but with one glaring difference - there was no opposition! Apparently the theory was that this allowed you to work on various moves and 'zonal play' without the interference of the other team.

The first of these 'matches' took place one morning at Roker Park with a rather bemused Sunderland first eleven lining up ready for kick-off. As I recall Dave Swindlehurst got the match under way passing to Eric Gates who then played it to Mark Proctor out on the left wing.

A youthful Gordon Armstrong (8) looks on as Chris McMenemy takes this coaching session with the Sunderland youth team

David pushed it back to Alan Kennedy on the edge of our box, who turned and rolled it back to our goalkeeper, Iain Hesford. Unfortunately, at that precise moment Iain happened to be placing his cap at the foot of the post and turned to see the ball rolling past him and into the net - one-nil down in the first minute and we weren't even playing anybody!

## I can still see Lawrie walking back to the centre circle shaking his head in disbelief and muttering: 'Bloody hell, we're even beating ourselves now!'

# Lawrie sacked!

Any support Lawrie had on the Roker terraces evaporated early in his second campaign in charge and it came as no surprise when his tenure as Sunderland manager came to an end. The fans were rightly furious that the season had once again ended in a relegation dog-fight and their frustration finally boiled over after a 2-1 home defeat against Sheffield United when an angry mob besieged the players' entrance immediately after the game. Within a matter of hours Lawrie had gone, packing his bags and heading south with his family, literally overnight - it was a sad end to what had promised to be a very special era in the club's history.

**We had a brief conversation just before he left during which he said: 'Gary, make sure you do everything in your power to ensure this club isn't relegated'. Contrary to popular belief I think Lawrie was desperate to succeed at Sunderland and was as disappointed as anyone when things didn't work out. As a person, I really liked the man and I'll always be grateful to him for making me club captain. In retrospect, perhaps he made a big mistake leaving Southampton - he had created something special there which he tried to replicate at Sunderland, but failed.**

With the trap-door to Division 3 now creaking open perilously, our new chairman Bob Murray turned to Bob Stokoe, the man the fans had named 'The Messiah' after he had led Sunderland to that magnificent FA Cup victory in 1973. With only seven games remaining perhaps 'divine intervention' was now our only hope!

I got on great with Bob, a real football man and also a smashing guy even though he always insisted on calling me 'Gordon'! In fairness, he'd been given little time to turn things around but two wins and two draws meant for the second year running we went into our final game of the season knowing victory would secure our second Division status.

On this occasion, Barnsley were the visitors to Roker Park and for the first half hour or so it looked as though we'd slaughter them as we raced to a two goal lead as well as missing goodness knows how many chances. Then, just before half-time, Barnsley pulled one back with a speculative 20-yard effort which screamed into the top corner. The turning point came early in the second half when we were awarded a penalty after Eric Gates had been upended in the box. It was the chance to make the game safe but when Mark Proctor's shot was saved, the game turned dramatically.

After that it was 'panic stations' as the visitors took control and despite some desperate defending we conceded twice in the closing stages to end up losing 3-2. It was a game that should have been a formality but we'd blown it and results elsewhere meant that we'd finished the season third from bottom and were now in the dreaded play-offs.

# the 'Messiah' is back

# The blackest day...

In football, most players will experience their fair share of highs and lows, great moments that will live with you forever and those horrible games that give you nightmares for years - unfortunately our play-off games against Gillingham, particularly the second leg at Roker Park, fall into the latter category. A 3-2 defeat in the first-leg at the Priestfield Stadium was certainly disappointing but we were still confident we could win the tie, particularly with away goals counting double which meant a 1-0 victory in the home leg would see us through.

The Roker Park game was scheduled for the Sunday immediately after the FA Cup final, which was a major blow for me personally as my brother Dave was playing for Coventry City against Spurs in the game at Wembley. From being kids at home in Manchester our football careers had developed almost in parallel and I was desperate to be there to give him my support from the stands. However, with our preparation for the Gillingham game being so vital, I was forced to settle for watching the game on television as Coventry upset all the odds by beating Spurs 3-2 with Dave scoring their opening goal. As I watched him parading the cup around the stadium in front of the ecstatic Sky Blue hordes, I couldn't help thinking that perhaps the stage was now set for a double celebration in the Bennett household!

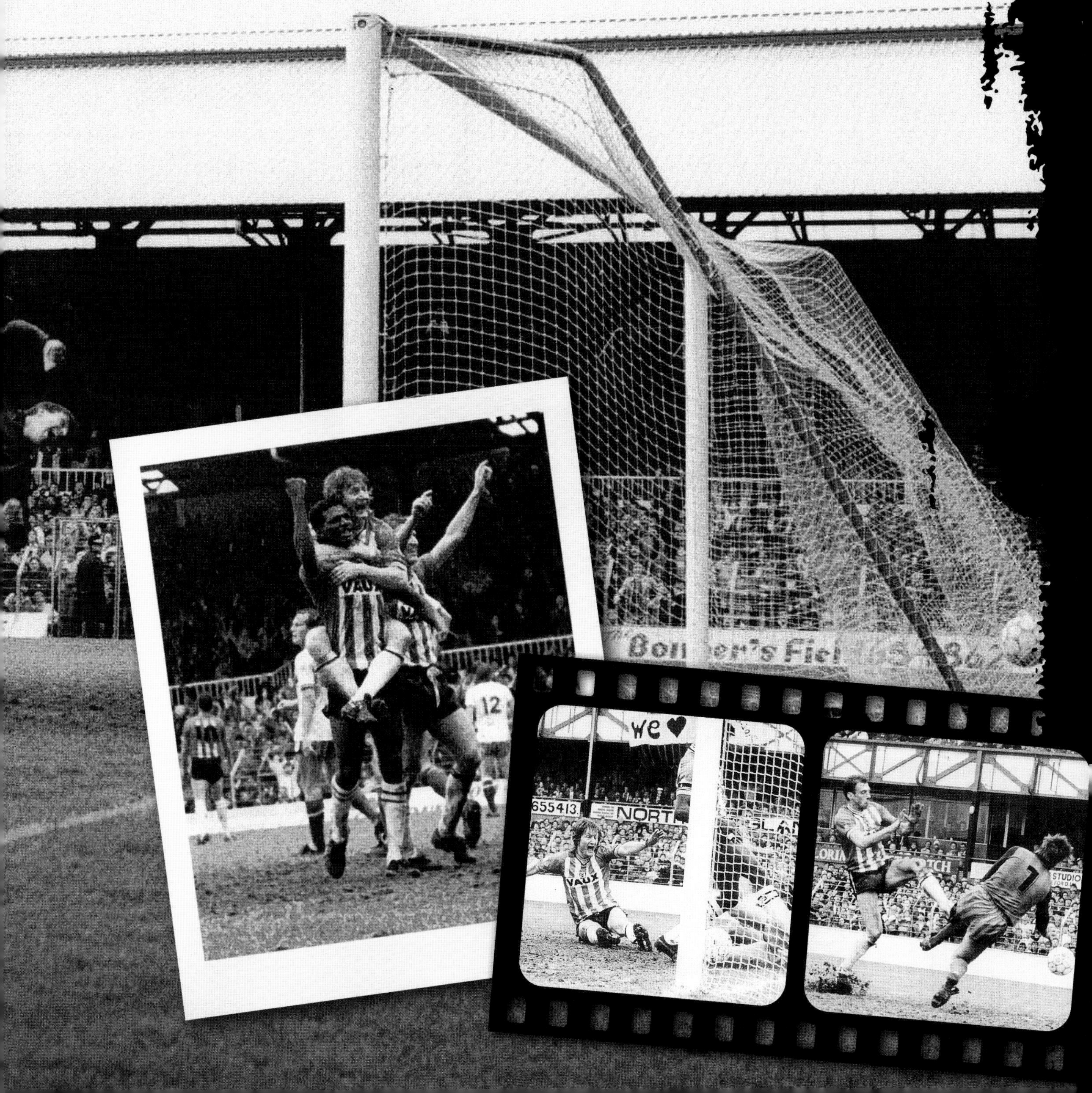
VAUX
655413
we
VAUX

Keeping a clean sheet had been a problem for us all season and so it proved in the second leg when we conceded early in the first half. Despite another missed penalty from Mark Proctor, two goals from Eric Gates kept our hopes alive but with the game entering the final minutes, scores were level at 2-2 or more importantly, we were 5-4 down on aggregate. In desperation, I'd pushed forward hoping to get on the end of something when, with our last attack of the 90 minutes, the ball was played in from the left and I managed to beat their defender in the air and send a looping header over the keeper and into the net - needless to say, Roker Park erupted!

The pendulum had swung back dramatically in our favour but yet again our destiny would hinge on a penalty, this time for Gillingham. There was a huge roar when Iain Hesford saved the kick but in the aftermath that followed they managed force the ball over the line. Keith Bertschin gave us hope with a diving header deep in extra-time but as the final whistle blew it was the Gillingham players and fans who were celebrating. It was a cruel way to go - we'd won the game 4-3 but the away goals rule had put us down.

**The players were naturally gutted but for our wonderful fans, it must have been so much worse. Players come and go but true supporters stay for ever and as their captain, I was heartbroken for them.**

## Over the years the fans had suffered their fair share of disappointments but without any shadow of a doubt, this was their blackest day.

The goal that clinched promotion - Marco heads it down, Gatesy fires it home and the lads go crazy!

As a player, Denis Smith was never short of confidence in his own ability and it was largely due to his own self-belief that our chairman, Bob Murray, was able to clinch the deal that saw the former Stoke City defender take over the manager's chair at Roker Park in the summer of 1987.

At the time, Denis was at York City having taken his first steps into management four years earlier and was seen by Sunderland as a man ideally placed to turn the club's fortunes around, not least because of his vast experience in the lower leagues. When Sunderland made their approach however, City immediately demanded £40,000 compensation, a major stumbling block for our cash-strapped club. Eventually, a somewhat unusual compromise was reached when it was agreed that Sunderland would make an initial down payment of £20,000 with Denis agreeing to pay City £10,000 out of his own money if he failed to lead Sunderland to promotion within two years!

With Sunderland almost broke following relegation, our new boss was forced to 'wheel and deal' in the transfer market and whilst the sale of Mark Proctor to Sheffield Wednesday for £265,000 helped boost the club's coffers, it was clear that the days of big money, high profile signings were a thing of the past at Roker Park.

The first new players to arrive were John McPhail, a solid and vastly experienced central-defender and full-back John Kay who joined the club from Wimbledon. At Plough Lane, John had been a member of the legendary 'Crazy Gang', a nickname earned by the team following their wild antics and tough, uncompromising approach on the park, 'qualities' that John had in abundance which, not surprisingly, soon made him a great favourite with the Roker faithful!

Then, after a somewhat indifferent start to our first season in Division 3, we heard that Denis had returned to York City to sign a young striker by the name of Marco Gabbiadini. With a name like that it wasn't difficult to conjure up a picture of a dark, bronzed Italian superstar so, as you can imagine, there were more than a few comments flying around the Roker Park dressing-room when this pale blonde kid walked in for his first morning's training!

Marco with admirers - Sunderland
fans meet our new striker shortly
after his arrival from York City

Champions!

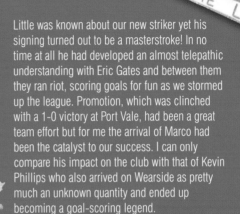

Little was known about our new striker yet his signing turned out to be a masterstroke! In no time at all he had developed an almost telepathic understanding with Eric Gates and between them they ran riot, scoring goals for fun as we stormed up the league. Promotion, which was clinched with a 1-0 victory at Port Vale, had been a great team effort but for me the arrival of Marco had been the catalyst to our success. I can only compare his impact on the club with that of Kevin Phillips who also arrived on Wearside as pretty much an unknown quantity and ended up becoming a goal-scoring legend.

# What a difference a year makes!

Twelve months earlier our fans had left Roker Park after our final home game totally devastated, this time they were celebrating the Third Division title. The lads enjoyed every minute parading the trophy around the ground following our 3-1 victory over Northampton Town but more than that, we were absolutely delighted to give our magnificent supporters something to celebrate at long last.

Eric and Marco - The 'G Force'!

# The party continues!

Thousands travelled down to Rotherham for our final game of the season and, whilst there was nothing at stake we made sure we rewarded them with a victory, winning the game comfortably by four goals to one.

**It was a carnival atmosphere throughout with our fans, who were packed into the tiny stand behind the goal at the low end of Rotherham's sloping pitch, enjoying every minute.**

I remember our third goal came from a penalty but before John McPhail could take the kick, one of our supporters clambered over the fence, raced onto the pitch and hammered the ball into the net past a bemused Rotherham keeper!

Celebrating with our fans packed into the tiny stand behind the goal at Millmoor. l to r: Steve Doyle, Marco Gabbiadini, yours truly, Gordon Armstrong, Keith Bertschin, Frank Gray, John McPhail, John Kay, Steve Smelt & Viv Busby

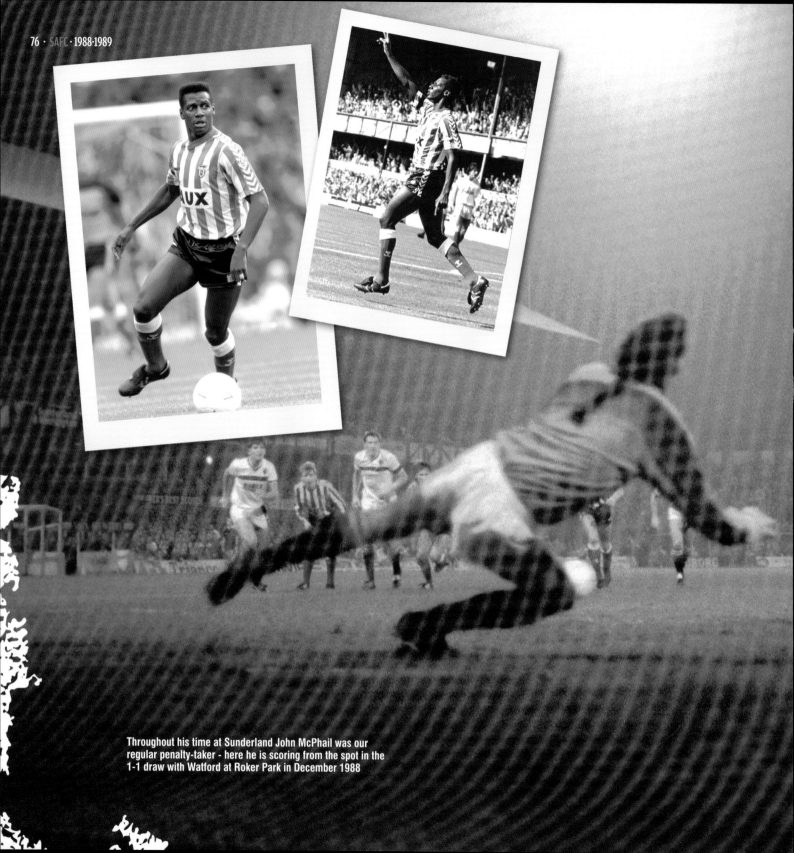

Throughout his time at Sunderland John McPhail was our
regular penalty-taker - here he is scoring from the spot in the
1-1 draw with Watford at Roker Park in December 1988

There's no question that promotion was our main priority when the 1989-90 campaign kicked off and whilst a decent run in the cup competitions is always good for the confidence our foray into the League Cup that season will always be remembered

# for all the wrong reasons...

Having beaten Fulham and Bournemouth in the earlier rounds, we were then drawn away to Fourth Division Exeter City. Progress to the next stage of the competition appeared to be a formality however, with only ten minutes or so of the game remaining we found ourselves two goals down and a real upset seemed to be on the cards. It was one of those games when we just didn't manage to get going and with the home side totally in command we seemed to be on our way out of the competition. Fortunately, a late rally saved the day as goals from Gordon Armstrong and Eric Gates secured an unlikely draw and a replay back at Roker.

It was hardly a result to celebrate and whilst one or two of the lads decided to head into town to sample the local nightspots, I was more than happy to turn in for a good night's sleep in readiness for the long journey home the following day. It must have been around three in the morning when I was awoken by the night porter, summoning me to reception saying:

**'You'll have to come down Mr. Bennett, all hell's broken out - some of the Sunderland players have been on the rampage walking on car roofs and such like and they've ended up in the police cells!'**

I was club captain and the porter explained that he felt it was better to ring me rather than disturb our manager, Denis Smith. As far as I could ascertain, John Kay and Paul Williams were the main culprits and had been accused of damaging cars in the local neighbourhood whilst walking back to our hotel. The following morning the hotel reception was crawling with the national press eager to pick up on the scandal. Eventually, the lads were released with John Kay taking the blame, mainly to protect Paul Williams who at the time was only a youngster starting out in the game - it was a great gesture and typical of Kaysey, a real character and one of the nicest guys you could ever wish to meet.

Tony Norman, Peter Davenport and I bringing the beer with one of the legendary Vaux Brewery drays!

As part of the club's economy drive during the 1990s
all the lads were expected to undertake additional duties...

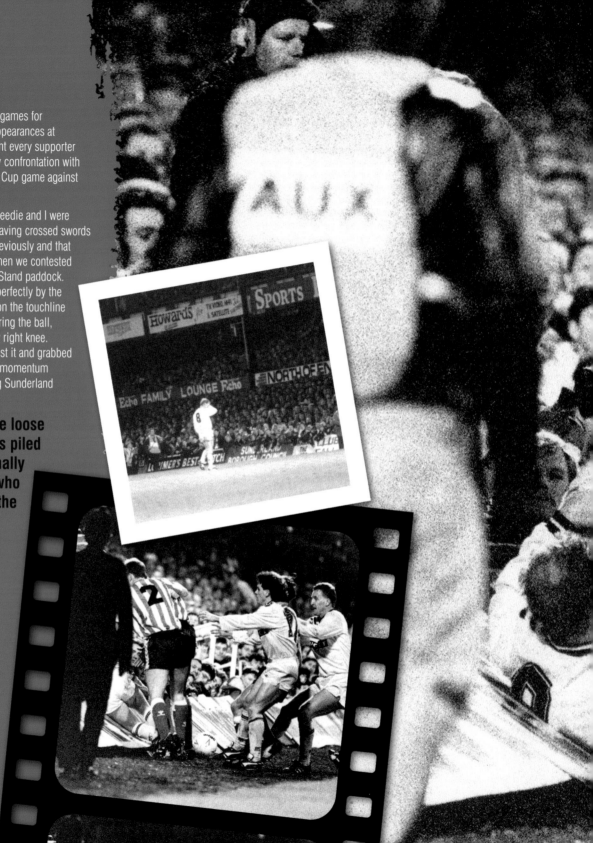

I ended up playing over 400 games for Sunderland including four appearances at Wembley, yet the one incident every supporter still wants to talk about is my confrontation with David Speedie in the League Cup game against Coventry City at Roker Park.

As I've mentioned earlier, Speedie and I were hardly on the best of terms having crossed swords on a number of occasions previously and that night it all came to a head when we contested the ball in front of the Clock Stand paddock. The incident was picked up perfectly by the television cameras perched on the touchline as Speedie, completely ignoring the ball, took a deliberate lunge at my right knee. To be honest, I completely lost it and grabbed him around the throat as our momentum carried us towards the baying Sunderland fans in the paddock.

**Momentarily, all hell broke loose as players from both sides piled in and when order was finally restored the City striker, who had been pinned against the perimeter fence under a deluge of bodies, looked visibly shaken, sitting on the cinder track trying to regain his composure.**

Yet again I was heading for an early bath although on this occasion, as the television replay clearly showed, I had every right to feel aggrieved.

# Speedie exit!

# The Play-offs
## semi-final 1st leg

Throughout the season promotion always seemed within reach yet we rarely looked like clinching one of the automatic promotion spots. Instead we had to settle for a sixth place finish and a place in the play-offs against, of all teams, our arch rivals Newcastle United.

## If ever the stage was set for a 'battle royal', then this was it!

The first leg at Roker Park was a dour game with few chances for either side and seemed to be heading for a goal-less draw when, with only minutes remaining, we were awarded a controversial penalty. Marco was racing into the Fulwell End penalty area and when he was brought down by Mark Stimson, the referee had no hesitation in pointing to the spot. It was a decision that infuriated the United players who surrounded the official in protest but, from where I was standing it did look a clear penalty.

**Paul Hardyman, who had become our regular penalty-taker since joining us from Portsmouth earlier in the season, was entrusted with the spot-kick. It was a pressure moment for Paul and you could almost hear a pin drop as he stepped up to take the kick. Unfortunately, John Burridge diving low to his right managed to parry his shot and as the ball broke clear Paul raced in for the rebound only to be beaten to it by the United 'keeper. In his frustration, Paul carried through leaving Burridge rolling around in agony with the United players piling in for revenge.**

To be honest, Paul had given the referee little choice and was immediately sent off. Moments later the final whistle blew and, as the United players raced to the Roker End to join their supporters in celebration, we trooped off to the dressing-room where Paul was sitting, heartbroken and inconsolable. His biggest frustration was that he was now banned for the second leg and therefore wouldn't get the opportunity to make amends.

Sunderland fans hold their breath, but Paul Hardyman misses from the spot with only minutes remaining and the pendulum swings in the Magpies favour

# Sunderland 0  Newcastle United 0

# the 'G-Force' at their very best!

Newcastle defender Mark Stimson is unable to stop Marco slotting home the decisive second goal

The all-important first goal from Eric Gates

Newcastle fans sporting in defeat!

# The Play-offs
### semi-final 2nd leg
## Newcastle United 0  Sunderland 2

Not surprisingly, the bookies had now installed the Magpies as red-hot favourites to go through to the final at Wembley, yet we were quietly confident of getting a result having played quite well away from home throughout the season. What we needed more than anything to tilt the tie back in our favour was an early goal and 13 minutes into the game it duly arrived. Gary Owers was the architect, attacking down the right and crossing to the near post where Gatesy raced in as brave as ever to force the ball over the line.

The goal had clearly stunned the home crowd and as the game moved into the second half you could hear the frustration beginning to rain down from the terraces. Mind you, that was nothing compared to their reaction when we scored again with only five minutes remaining. Again Eric Gates was involved but this time as the provider with a pin-point return pass to release Marco into the box to drive home a terrific left-foot shot just inside the far post - it was the 'G-Force' at their very best!

With our fans behind the Leazes End goal celebrating in ecstasy, it all became just too much for many home supporters to take and they poured onto the pitch in their hundreds. Soon the scenes became quite ugly as they raced towards our fans at the opposite end of ground with stewards and police fighting desperately to keep them at bay leaving referee George Courtney no choice but to lead the players back to sanctuary of the dressing-rooms. There was now a very real possibility that the game would be abandoned and there was an agonising wait for us until George appeared at the dressing-room door stating: 'Don't worry lads, if we have to stay here all night I'll make sure this game is finished!' After a delay of around 20 minutes the pitch was finally cleared and we were able go out and finish the game although none of us hung around too long when the final whistle blew!

**Not surprisingly, the Newcastle players were distraught and in the players' lounge afterwards one or two were moaning about how unfair the play-off system was and that having finished in third place, they should have been promoted automatically. Needless to say, we were less than sympathetic!**

It was around mid-night when were arrived back on Wearside where the whole town was alive with celebrating Sunderland fans and we were given little choice but to join in although most of the lads didn't need too much persuasion, I can assure you. I can remember the first couple of night clubs but after that it's all a bit of a blur!

On the 28th May 1990 came one of the proudest moments of my entire football career when I led out the Sunderland team to meet Swindon Town in the Second Division Play-Off final at Wembley. People tell me I was the first black player to lead a club side out at the famous old ground and if that's the case, then I'm doubly proud.

**As for the game itself, it was a huge disappointment from a Sunderland perspective and almost a mirror image of the Milk Cup Final five years earlier where we had failed to perform on the day and lost to an own goal. In 1985, Gordon Chisholm was the unlucky player, this time it was my turn!**

In fairness to Swindon they could have been a couple of goals ahead before Alan McLaughlin hit a speculative shot from outside the box which took a wicked deflection off my shins and ballooned over a helpless Tony Norman in our goal. Thereafter we never looked like getting back into the game and could have lost by a much heavier score-line had it not been for Tony who was absolutely brilliant producing a string of truly stunning saves to deny the opposition.

Quite why we failed to perform in such an important game is hard to say although our cause certainly wasn't helped when Marco limped off injured midway through the second-half. He'd been struggling with an injury leading up to the final and with hindsight, perhaps he shouldn't have played, although I could fully understand why Denis decided to take the risk. On their day the 'G Force' partnership was almost unstoppable and Marco in particular was the sort of player who could explode into action and win the game for you with a touch of sheer brilliance.

# The Play-off Final

Swindon Town captain Colin Calderwood and I pose for the cameras just before kick-off

Yet again Wembley had proved to be an unhappy hunting ground for us but this time salvation was just around the corner. Leading up to the final there had been one or two articles in the press regarding an F.A. enquiry into Swindon's finances although at the time I gave the stories no more than a passing glance.

**In the days immediately after the final however, the rumours began to gather momentum and about a week later the news broke that Swindon were to be relegated having been found guilty of financial irregularities and we, as losing finalists, would be promoted in their place.**

We were in the top flight again, albeit by the most unlikely of routes - the question now was, were we good enough to stay there?

I can't believe it! Alan McLaughlin's shot has just deflected off my shins and past Tony Norman for the only goal of the game

# One of the great moments!

**As a true-blue Manchester City fan born and bred, I always relished putting one over on our arch rivals, but to score the winning goal against the Red Devils with only minutes remaining really is the stuff of dreams!**

I remember the goal as if it were yesterday - the scores were level with only minutes remaining when I managed to win possession off Gary Pallister near the left wing corner flag, which caught the United defence by surprise and left me with a clear run on goal. It was a tight angle, but as Les Sealey advanced I managed to curl a right foot shot past him and into the net just inside the far post. It was an unbelievable moment with the crowd going absolutely crazy as we celebrated in front of the main stand.

**Having gained promotion through the 'back door' the previous season, I suppose it was no surprise when our first season back in the top flight turned out to be another fight for survival and yet again our fate was to be decided on the final day of the season with an away fixture at Manchester City, of all places!**

The battle to avoid the drop had ended up as a two horse race with Luton Town, who were due to face already relegated Derby County at Kenilworth Road. Not surprisingly, 'The Hatters' had been installed as favourites to survive, although our hopes were raised when we heard that Wearside-born Mick Harford would be leading County's attack.

An estimated 15,000 fans had travelled down from Wearside and the support they gave us that afternoon compares with anything I ever experienced during my time with the club. From the moment we ran out onto the Maine Road pitch right up to the final whistle and beyond, they were quite magnificent.

**Ironically, it was none other than Niall Quinn who turned out to be the architect of our destruction, although in an amazing few minutes just before the break it looked as though we might be in with a real chance. The big Irishman had given the home side the lead early on but we managed to draw level five minutes before the break with a thumping header from Marco following a great run and cross from John Kay. Almost immediately we won a corner on the right, which was only partially cleared and when the ball was played back in I managed to head home to put us in front. Our fans behind the goal were now going absolutely crazy and moments later another huge roar went up following the news that Mick Harford had scored at Kenilworth Road.**

Amazingly, the drama continued in whirlwind fashion with City snatching an equaliser right on the stroke of half-time when Gary Owers mistimed a clearance to set up Quinny who slotted home from close-range. It was mixed emotions as we trooped off for the interval, but things got considerably worse when entered the dressing room to be told that Luton were actually leading 1-0 - Mick Harford had scored alright but unfortunately for us, it had been an own goal!

We now faced an uphill battle and when we were denied a clear penalty early in the second half, I think we realised it wasn't going to be our day. Marco was sent clear in the box and when he rounded Margetson in the City goal he looked a certain scorer, but just as he was about to slot the ball into the empty net the keeper caught his trailing leg and he fired wide.

When the news filtered through that Luton were now leading 2-0 we knew we were down and David White's winner in the dying seconds was purely academic as far as we were concerned. It had been an incredible afternoon but ultimately a heartbreaking one and I couldn't help feeling for our wonderful fans. They had backed us to the hilt throughout the game and I'll never forget the reception they gave us at the end as Denis Smith led us across the park to thank them for their support.

**Denis was a tough character and certainly never one to show his emotions yet he was in tears as he walked down the tunnel.**

City's Colin Hendry and Niall Quinn try to infiltrate our defensive wall

# Relegation at Man City

Peter Davenport and Marco Gabbiadini are the first to congratulate me after I'd netted our second goal

On the beach at Roker following the launch of our new Hummel training kit

In 1991 the players had a 'worst dressed competition' to raise money for a Macmillan Nurses Appeal.
Back Row: (left to right) Steve Smelt, Tim Carter, Richard Ord, Brian Mooney, Tony Norman, Kevin Ball, Gary Owers, John Kay, Anthony Smith, Ian Sampson, Warren Hawke, John Byrne, Don Goodman, David Wales, Gary Bennett, Steve Gaughan, Brian Atkinson. Front Row: Wayne Walls, Paul Moore, Stephen Brodie, Peter Davenport, Gordon Armstrong, Paul Bracewell, Kieron Brady, Anton Rogan, Paul Hardyman, Martin Gray, Tony Cullen.

1992 also saw the opening of 'Boo-Ka', our flower shop in Sunderland town centre

Peter Davenport on target in the 3rd round tie against Port Vale

Malcolm Crosby

# Sackings,
# Signings
# and the FA Cup...

There's a saying in football management circles that the only sure thing about the job is that one day you'll get the sack and, apart from the odd exception, that's pretty much the case in what has to be football's most precarious profession.

It therefore came as no surprise when Denis Smith was relieved of his duties after a poor start to the 1991-92 campaign, however what I did find somewhat unusual were the circumstances surrounding his departure.

Earlier in the season the club had taken the decision to cash in on their prized asset, Marco Gabbiadini, and when Crystal Palace tabled a bid of £1.8 million it was an offer simply too good to refuse. The cash was immediately made available to Denis to fund a major team rebuilding programme and three new signings were soon added to our ranks. The first to arrive was Anton Rogan a central defender signed from Celtic and he was followed shortly afterwards by John Byrne, a player Denis had chased for some time and one who would make a significant impact in the season ahead. Finally, striker Don Goodman arrived from West Brom for fee of around £900,000 to complete the new-look Sunderland line-up.

Having allowed Denis to sign new players and effectively spend the club's entire transfer budget, it seemed that the directors had given him their backing for the campaign ahead yet within a matter of weeks he and his assistant Viv Busby were shown the door. It was a strange decision and speaking personally I was sorry to see them leave, particularly bearing in mind that the club was on the verge of slipping into the oblivion of the lower leagues when they arrived five years earlier.

**Football management is a tough profession and getting back into the game isn't always easy, although Viv would face a much greater fight a few years later when he was diagnosed with leukaemia. Thankfully, after a long battle, he made a full recovery and is still involved in the game as assistant manager of Workington Reds.**

Following the departure of Denis and Viv, reserve team coach Malcolm Crosby was handed the job of caretaker manager although at the time, no one could have imagined that by the end of the season he would be installed in the post on a permanent basis.

If the newspapers were to be believed, the club had firmly set their sights on an established top-name manager yet once we'd set off on a decent run in the FA Cup, Malcolm's chances of landing the job began to increase dramatically as each round passed.

**Victories over Port Vale and Oxford had taken us into the 5th round although a 1-1 draw against West Ham at Roker Park left us with a difficult task in the replay at Upton Park. However, on the night we produced an outstanding performance winning a tremendous end to end cup-tie by the odd goal in five with John Byrne bagging a brace and young David Rush netting the winner from a Kieron Brady cross.**

Kieron was one of the most talented players I ever played with and he reminded me very much of John Robertson, Forest's Scottish international winger. Like Robertson, Kieron was stockily built and lacked any real pace but on his day he could destroy defenders with pure skill. West Ham were certainly aware of him having lost a seven goal thriller at Roker the previous season when Kieron produced one of his best performances for the club. Sadly, a vascular condition forced him to quit the game in November 1993.

*Brian Atkinson and David Rush battle it out at Upton Park*

**Viv Busby**

*Tony Norman pulls off a stunning save to deny the Hammers*

When the 6th round draw paired us with Chelsea at Stamford Bridge,
memories of 1985 when we dumped them out of the Milk Cup came flooding back.

John Byrne heads our equaliser
in the 1-1 draw at Stamford Bridge

Thankfully however, there was no repeat of the
riots we had to endure seven years earlier and
a solid performance earned us a 1-1 draw with
John Byrne netting our equaliser with a looping
header after Paul Bracewell's speculative lob
into the box.

The replay turned out
to be one of Roker Park's truly memorable
nights with John Byrne again in tremendous form setting up
Peter Davenport for a first half opener. As the game entered the
closing stages it looked as though that goal was going to be
enough to see us through then Dennis Wise latched onto a
Vinnie Jones pass to level the scores from close range. It was
a bitter blow and clearly the pendulum had now swung in the
visitors favour, yet in the final minutes we won the tie in the
most dramatic fashion imaginable with a glorious header from
Gordon Armstrong.

**We had won a corner on the right and when
Brian Atkinson floated over the cross, Gordon rose
to beat Andy Townsend and power a header low
into the bottom corner of the net with Dave Beasant
in the Chelsea goal beaten all ends up.**

I'll never forget the look of sheer ecstasy
on Gordon's face as he raced away with our
fans going wild with delight!

**Next up were Norwich City at Hillsborough and the opportunity for us to avenge the Milk Cup final defeat of 1985.**

The other semi-final was being contested between Liverpool and Portsmouth throwing up the very real possibility of an all Second Division final at Wembley. Naturally, a Pompey victory was what we were hoping for but first of all we had to overcome a pretty useful Norwich City side.

# The Red & White Army take over the Hillsborough terraces

SUNDERLAND · NORWICH CITY

FA CUP Semi FINAL

AT HILLSBOROUGH. SHEFFIELD ON SUNDAY. 5th APRIL. 1992. KICK-OFF 3.30 P.M.

Throughout the cup run John Byrne had been our talisman with some stirring performances up front and it was clear to see why Denis Smith had rated him so highly.

John had scored in every round so far and midway through the first half he continued his record, heading home Brian Atkinson's cross from close range. After that there was little between the sides although to be fair we were never in any real danger - having said that, the last five minutes or so did seem to last an eternity!

**Sheffield Wednesday FC**

*************************************
*********** F. A. CUP - SEMI-FINAL
*                SUNDERLAND
*                  - V -
*        SOUTHAMPTON or NORWICH CITY
*************************************
*********** SUNDAY 5th APRIL 1992
            Kick - off 3.30pm

            KOP - SUNDERLAND

BLOCK    GANGWAY ROW    SEAT    PRICE
                                 9.00

            STANDING ONLY

           THIS PORTION TO BE RETAINED

**The scoreboard says it all, 1-0 up with only seconds remaining and not surprisingly, John Kay is in no hurry to take this throw-in**

**There were amazing scenes at the end with everyone, players, backroom staff and supporters alike, going absolutely crazy. For Malcolm Crosby in particular, it must have been an incredible feeling - less than six months earlier he had been looking after the reserve team at Roker and now he was about to lead Sunderland out in the FA Cup final at Wembley!**

As we headed back home to Wearside our opponents for the biggest game in our careers were still unknown. The other semi-final had ended in a 1-1 draw although Portsmouth almost pulled of a shock result having led through a Darren Anderton goal right up to the dying seconds when a controversial Ronnie Whelan penalty had rescued Liverpool. You rarely get a second chance against the big boys and so it proved in the replay at Villa Park although Pompey had ran the Merseysiders mighty close with the tie going to a penalty shoot-out, the first time a FA Cup semi-final had ever been settled in this way.

Thankfully unlike 1985, our preparations for the final weren't hampered by arguments over tickets, bonuses and sponsorship, although we did have the pressing business of Second Division survival to contend with having hovered around the lower reaches of the league for most of the season.

**When survival was secured with two games to go, Malcolm was installed as permanent boss.**

**Mam and Dad at Wembley about to watch one of their sons play in an FA Cup final for the third time**

**Paul Bracewell, Gary Owers and John Byrne** supervise the recording of our cup final record, **'Ain't no stopping us now'**

# We're on our way!..

SAFC · 1991-1992 · 109

WEMBLEY STADIUM

THE FOOTBALL ASSOCIATION
CHALLENGE CUP FINAL ME

SATURDAY 9TH MAY 1992
KICK-OFF 3.00 PM
PLEASE TAKE YOUR POSITIONS BY 2.15 PM
TURNSTILES OPEN AT 1.00 PM
Special items and conditions of issue apply
to this ticket. See the reverse.

TURNSTILE D
BLOCK     ROW          SEAT
105  31              158
FINALIST 1
£35.00
6   407 140492 105406A

**They don't come much bigger than Liverpool
at Wembley and whilst we started the game as rank outsiders, we took comfort
in the fact that 19 years earlier Sunderland had upset all the odds with an unlikely victory
over Leeds United, one of the top sides in English football at the time.**

Liverpool boss Graeme Souness had missed the semi-final drama following a heart by-pass operation but declared himself fit for
the final, although he settled for a seat on the bench allowing Ronnie Moran, his number two, to lead the team out alongside Malcolm Crosby.

Our game plan was to take the game to Liverpool and hopefully snatch an early goal, which would give us the psychological advantage just as Ian Porterfield's opener had in 1973.

**After 13 minutes the chance, and probably the defining moment of the game, duly arrived. We had won a corner on the right and when the ball was played in it dropped invitingly to John Byrne on the edge of the six-yard box, right in front of goal.**

It was the sort of opportunity John would stick away every day of the week in training but this time, when it really mattered, he completely missed his kick and the chance was gone. It was an agonising moment and one that would haunt him for years.

A heartbreaking moment - John Byrne misses a golden opportunity to give us the lead

The scores were still level at break and we had given a fair account of ourselves in a fairly even first half, but the game turned two minutes into the second period when Michael Thomas volleyed home following a run down the right by Steve McManaman.

**After that it really was an uphill battle and with Jan Molby orchestrating proceedings in the middle of the park, we found it almost impossible to get some decent possession. With 20 minutes left Ian Rush netted in typical fashion to settle the issue and effectively put an end to what for me personally was another miserable day at Wembley.**

Anton Rogan and I manage to win possession from Liverpool's Ray Houghton

I'd been to Wembley four times with Sunderland and ended up on the losing side on each occasion, although this time I did manage to finish up with a winner's medal, in fact all the Sunderland players did - there was a complete mix-up by the officials making the presentations and afterwards we ended up down on the pitch having to sort everything out with the Liverpool players who'd all been given loser's medals!

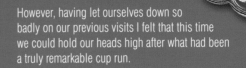

However, having let ourselves down so badly on our previous visits I felt that this time we could hold our heads high after what had been a truly remarkable cup run.

**Sure, we hadn't managed to conjure up a fairy tale ending in 1973 fashion but along the way our supporters had been treated to some unforgettable games and for once they could be proud of their team - this was borne out by the incredible reception they gave us when we returned home to Wearside a few days later.**

This diving header against Portsmouth during
the 1992-93 season was one of the best goals I'd ever scored.

**Unfortunately it was disallowed!**

Malcolm Crosby presents me with a cake
to celebrate my birthday

One of the proudest moments of my Sunderland career came in July 1993 when I led the team out for my testimonial game against Glasgow Rangers, the culmination of nine wonderful years at Roker Park.

My son Leon was at my side as I walked out onto the pitch to a guard of honour and the moment was captured in an oil painting specially commissioned by my Sunderland teammates which to this day remains one of my most treasured possessions.

An injury prevented Rangers star Ally McCoist from playing in my testimonial game, but I was delighted that the former Sunderland striker still took the trouble to come down from Scotland to lend his support.

SUNDERLAND A.F.C.
V
GLASGOW RANGERS

Gary Bennett

TESTIMONIAL MATCH

WEDNESDAY 28th JULY 1993 KICK-OFF 7.30pm

COMMEMORATIVE PROGRAMME

PRICE £1

With a renewed optimism now surrounding the club following our cup exploits the previous season, Malcolm wasted no time in making his first foray into the transfer market and by the time the new campaign got under way three new signings had been added to our ranks. John Colquhoun and Shaun Cunnington, both accomplished midfielders arrived in July and just before the start of the season Terry Butcher was brought in to add strength and experience to the defence.

**Terry was a massive figure in the game and had been part of Bobby Robson's great Ipswich Town side of the 1980s, picking up 77 caps for England along the way. I was 30 years-old with quite a bit of experience under my belt when he arrived, yet I learned so much playing alongside him in the centre of our defence. Apart from his sheer physical presence, his reading of game and positional play were incredible yet he could also mix it when required.**

I remember on one occasion, we were playing at Tranmere Rovers, who had former Celtic and Chelsea winger Pat Nevin playing out on the wing. Terry had played the latter part of his career at Rangers so whether there was any ill feeling carried over from their Old Firm encounters I'm not sure, but in one incident he sent the slightly built Rovers winger flying across the cinder track with a thunderous tackle, followed by a volley of verbal abuse for good measure!

Malcolm Crosby's rise to managerial stardom had been almost meteoric and his demise was equally swift when, after only eight months in the job, he was relieved of his duties. Results had certainly been poor, but it seemed to me the Sunderland board were just waiting for an excuse to show him the door. Ironically they chose to announce his sacking immediately after a 'Pools Panel' defeat at Tranmere Rovers, making a mockery of the club's credibility and inviting the inevitable derision from rival fans!

In all honesty, I don't think the directors really wanted to appoint Malcolm on a permanent basis in the first place, but the pressure from the fans and media following the cup run had probably left them with little choice. When Terry Butcher was appointed as his replacement within a matter of days, it merely fuelled speculation that he had been signed specifically for that purpose. It was common knowledge that the directors wanted a big name manager in charge and Terry certainly ticked all the boxes, yet his time in charge at Sunderland would be one of huge disappointment.

# Butch....

**I was out injured for most of the second half of the season and was forced to watch from the stands as the team continued to flirt with the very real possibility of another spell in Division 3 with our new boss seemingly unable to arrest the slide.**

His ritual cheer-leading at the end of each game may have appeased the fans but it had little impact on the team. There's no doubt Terry was trying everything in his power to turn things around and towards the end of the season, in preparation for our game at Newcastle, he took the squad on an assault course and then announced to the press that he was planning a commando-style raid on St James' Park during which we would steal the 3 points before the Magpies knew what had hit them. He even ordered the players to have their hair cropped short before the game so they would also look the part - unfortunately we lost 1·0!

I was back in the side by the time we headed to Notts County for the final game of the season with our Second Division status still very much in the balance. We needed a victory to be sure of staying up but the afternoon soon turned into a complete nightmare as we found ourselves three goals down at the interval. Kevin Ball pulled one back after the break but as the final whistle blew we found ourselves looking nervously to the terraces for an indication of results elsewhere. We knew we'd survived when our fans began pouring onto the pitch in celebration although after such an abject performance,

## I have to confess to feeling slightly embarrassed as they carried us off the park.

The following season, 1993-94, saw little improvement even though significant spending during the close season had seen Phil Gray, Andy Melville and Derek Ferguson added to our ranks. The fans were beginning to vent their feelings in no uncertain terms and a run of five consecutive defeats culminating in a 2-0 reverse at home to Southend United proved to be the last straw and Butcher was sacked immediately afterwards.

Mick Buxton, who Terry had brought to club some months earlier, was immediately installed as caretaker boss and quickly set about turning things around. Over the years he had established himself as one of the top managers in the lower leagues and had been linked with the Sunderland job on more than one occasion previously. I liked Mick enormously - he was a real grass roots football man, vastly experienced but with no airs or graces and I think the players responded to that. Certainly results improved dramatically and we were able finish the season in a comfortable mid-table position, helping to earn Mick the job on a permanent basis.

Sadly, we were unable to sustain that form the following season and with the all too familiar relegation clouds now beginning to gather over Roker Park as the season reached its climax, Mick's relatively short reign in charge came to an end. The axe fell after a 2-0 mid-week defeat at Barnsley and just to compound matters, the club were fined for playing an ineligible player, Dominic Matteo, whose registration hadn't been received at Football League headquarters by the required time!

**Nothing, it seemed, was going right for us yet within a few days the directors would appoint the man who would turn the club's fortunes around in the most dramatic fashion imaginable.**

# Buxton...

METRO FM 971 · Cellnet.

# ...and Reidy

From the moment Peter Reid first walked out onto the Roker Park pitch with his clenched fist raised in a gesture of defiance, you could sense that something inspirational was in the air. However, few supporters could have imagined that his arrival at the club would turn out to be the catalyst for a period of success the like of which hadn't been experienced since the glory days of 1973!

Initially, Peter had been appointed on a short term contract and his brief, quite simply, was to keep the club in Division One, not the easiest of tasks considering our perilous position near the foot of the table. His impact however, was immediate as a late Craig Russell strike earned us the points in his first game in charge against Sheffield United although the real turning point came a few of weeks later when we met fellow strugglers Swindon Town at Roker Park. It was a game we simply had to win and whilst it was a battle right through to the final whistle, Martin Smith's first-half volley proved to be enough to win the match and effectively guarantee our survival with matches to spare. I'd been left out for the Swindon game and whilst I didn't realise it at the time, it soon became apparent that I would never play for Sunderland again.

The following season saw 'Reid's Revival' really take off as the team stormed up the table, winning the league and promotion to the Premiership in spectacular fashion. It had been a remarkable turnaround, achieved largely with the squad that could very easily have been relegated the year before, although it was clear from the start of the campaign that I didn't figure in Peter's plans.

I could have stayed at the club and seen my contract out, but I was desperate to play regular first team football and whilst it was a massive wrench to leave Sunderland, I took the decision purely for football reasons.

**Carlisle United was the first club on the scene when their flamboyant chairman and owner Michael Knighton got in touch. Some years earlier he'd hit the headlines when it was widely reported that he was about to buy Manchester United no less, in fact he even got as far walking out onto the Old Trafford pitch to meet the fans and then proceeded to demonstrate his footballing prowess by juggling a ball in front of a packed Stretford End!**

Basically, Michael agreed that Carlisle would take over my Sunderland contract which still had nine months or so to run and the fact that I could continue living in Sunderland and commute to Cumbria each day suited me perfectly. Mick Wadsworth was in charge of team affairs at Brunton Park and had led the team to the Third Division championship the year before but they were now struggling to adapt to the higher level of football, so once again I found myself embroiled in a relegation battle! With little improvement in results, Mick ended up resigning midway through the campaign and despite a brave fight we finished fourth from bottom, missing out on survival by just three points.

I could easily have stayed on at Brunton Park where I was enjoying my football enormously, but once my contract had expired Michael Knighton was only prepared to offer me significantly reduced terms.

It was a difficult decision, then out of the blue I received a phone call from Mick Wadsworth telling me he'd just taken over as manager of Scarborough and asking whether I would be interested in joining him there.

*Michael Knighton performs to the Stretford End*

Martin Smith on the attack in the crucial relegation battle against Swindon Town at Roker Park

**Having just finished second bottom in the fourth tier of English football, Scarborough's future prospects could hardly have been described as optimistic, yet talking to Mick Wadsworth as he outlined his plans for the season that lay ahead left me in no doubt that I was making the right decision joining the east coast club.**

I was Mick's first signing since he'd taken over the manager's job but I was soon joined by my old Sunderland team-mate John Kay and midway through the season strikers Stephen Brodie and Chris Tate were added to the list of Roker old boys now plying their trade at the McCain Stadium. We were all still living on Wearside so each day the four of us would share a car and make the hour or so drive down the Yorkshire coast to Scarborough for training.

That first season was always going to be one of consolidation and a satisfactory 12th place finish gave us sufficient confidence to contemplate a serious promotion challenge the following season. Whilst an automatic promotion place always seemed just beyond us we did reach the play-offs but were soundly beaten by Torquay in the semi-finals.

I had two fantastic years at Scarborough scoring 20-odd goals into the bargain, which must have attracted the attention of my old mate David Hodgson who was managing Darlington at the time and when they tabled a £20,000 bid for my services I suddenly found myself heading back to the North East.

Andy Ritchie looks on as I get a header on target
during a league encounter at the McCain Stadium

## The F.A. Coaches & Managers Course 1997

With so many familiar faces in the frame, this photo looks more like a 'Who's Who' of English league managers.

There are over 100 in total but apart from myself, only one other black player - Cyrille Regis.

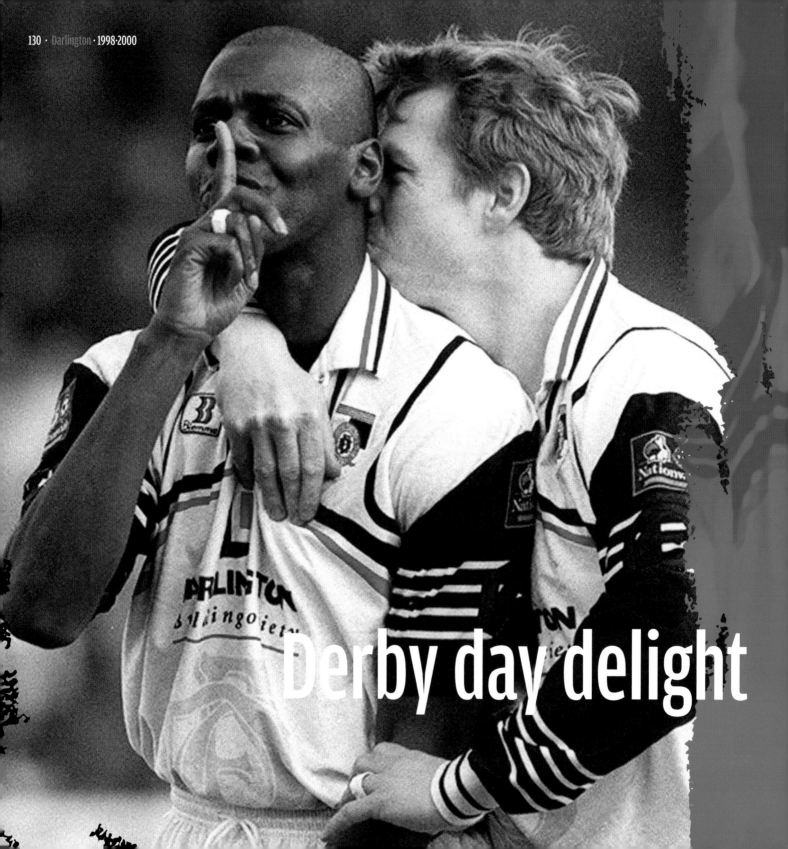

# Derby day delight

One of the high spots of my time with Darlington was scoring a cracking 20-yarder in the first couple of minutes of our local derby with our arch rivals Hartlepool United at Victoria Park. During my time with Sunderland I'd experienced quite a few Wear-Tyne derbies where the atmosphere at times bordered on pure hatred between rival fans and, whilst the numbers may have been considerably less, the rivalry between Darlo and Hartlepool was just as intense.

**In the photo opposite I'm celebrating silencing the home fans with that early strike while my teammate Marco Gabbiadini joins in the fun - we were always good pals during our time together at Roker Park although he's possibly taking things just a little bit too far on this occasion!**

We won this particular game 3-2 but the following season recorded an even greater victory over Hartlepool when we met in the Division 3 Play-Off semi-final. A 2-0 victory in the first leg at Victoria Park set us on our way and then a single goal win at Feethams sent our fans home in raptures looking forward to a trip to Wembley.

To be honest, we should have won automatic promotion comfortably that year, but a poor finish to the campaign meant we had to settle for third place. It was pretty much the same story in the final against Peterborough when we dominated the game, missed countless chances and ended up losing to the only goal of the game 15 minutes from time.

I hadn't figured in any of the play-off games and at 38-years-old it was pretty clear my playing career in league football was coming to an end.

**For some time I had been concentrating more on the coaching side of the game although any thoughts of a step into management seemed a million miles away when I suddenly received a phone call from our chairman George Reynolds offering me the job at Feethams.**

Football has always attracted more than its fair share of extrovert characters but I can honestly say that in all my years in the game I've never come across anyone quite like George Reynolds. A self-confessed safe-cracker who had spent quite a number of years behind bars in his younger days, it was often alleged that he had made much of his estimated £300 million fortune by, shall we say, somewhat dubious means! That said, he was still one hell of a businessman and his thriving kitchen worktop business in Shildon stood testament to his undoubted ability in the commercial world.

**George was born on Wearside and some years earlier had apparently been linked with a takeover bid for Sunderland Football Club although, like Michael Knighton, he was eventually forced to settle for a smaller club. His takeover at Darlington had happened almost overnight and he would often joke: 'I went out to buy a new car but ended up coming home with a football club!'**

No one could accuse George of lacking ambition though and with plans for a new 25,000 all-seater stadium already on the drawing board he was soon predicting Premiership football for the Quakers within five years! Throughout all this George was also embroiled with the authorities over various financial irregularities although it didn't seem to bother him too much if fact, I remember on one occasion he arranged a press call at Feethams one morning and then turned up wearing a prisoner's uniform just for their benefit!

The Benno & Monty managerial partnership

Perhaps it wasn't the best scenario for a young coach starting out in management but I'd always got on quite well with George and didn't envisage any real problems. My first job was to find a number two and I was delighted when my old mate Jim Montgomery, who was goalkeeping coach at Feethams, agreed to take the job. As ex-Sunderland players, Jim and I had been good friends for a number of years and I knew his vast experience in the game would be invaluable although, perhaps more importantly, he was also someone I knew I could trust.

**Initially, things were going really well with the team on the fringe of the play-offs, but it soon became apparent that George was going to be a somewhat difficult character to work for as he began to question virtually every decision we made. Jim and I were working around the clock to try and make a success of our first step into management but we couldn't help feeling that our chairman was doing his level best to undermine our positions at every opportunity. Eventually, Jim decided he'd had enough and resigned which was a huge disappointment to me although in all fairness I couldn't blame him.**

Then, just after the start of my second season in charge I began to hear rumours that George was going to bring in a new manager. At first it was only little snippets of information that were being bandied around but the stories soon gathered momentum when it was revealed that George was in discussions with former Orient boss Tommy Taylor. Whether Taylor was putting himself forward for the job I'm not sure, but my position as manager was clearly becoming untenable and eventually George called me into his office to give me the bad news. At the time I thought he'd made a big mistake and looking back at Tommy Taylor's record at the club, I've no reason to change that view.

A winter training session with T

Training on the banks of the River Wear under the picturesque backdrop of Durham Cathedral and Castle

George Reynolds was always one to attract publicity

Looking out over Feethams shortly after appointed as Darlington manager

My first taste of football management had been a bitter pill to swallow and apart from a brief six month spell working alongside Neil McNab down at Exeter, I've never once considered trying to get back into what has to be the game's toughest profession. Long days, constant pressure and untold criticism and abuse when things aren't going well - who needs it?

Spreading the word with John Anderson, Curtis Fleming and Leroy Rosenior

Niall Quinn, a long-term patron of 'Show Racism the Red Card', was elected to our Hall of Fame at a special presentation at the Stadium of Light in October 2008. Dave Anderson MP; Mayor of Sunderland Leslie Scott, and in this photo are and my old Sunderland teammate Kieron Brady

# now cism the Red Card

I first became involved in 'Show Racism the Red Card' shortly after it was formed in 1996 by Ged Grebby and Kevin Miles, Newcastle United fans who had become appalled at the level of racial abuse they were witnessing at just about every ground they visited following the Magpies. Ged was already an active member of 'Youth Against Racism in Europe', which sent out educational packs to schools and one of these got into the hands of Newcastle goalkeeper Shaka Hislop who promptly donated £50 to effectively launch the new campaign.

**I was interviewed for the very first film made by SRtRC and soon began attending various events to help educate young people against racism. In 2003 I was delighted to join the campaign on a full-time basis as head coach and together with John Anderson, Curtis Fleming and Dean Gordon we have continued to visit schools throughout the North East running anti-racism workshops together with football coaching for all ages and abilities.**

From those humble beginnings in 1996, the SRtRC campaign has grown beyond all recognition and apart from our headquarters in Whitley Bay, we now have offices in Glasgow and Cardiff as well as Ireland, Sweden, Denmark and Finland. The progress made has been truly phenomenal with racial abuse from the fans on the terraces now reduced dramatically. This is particularly noticeable at the top level where all-seater stadia and camera surveillance now allow identification of the offenders almost instantly, a far cry from the days of the open terraces when all levels of abuse would rain down on black players with the authorities unable and often it seemed, unwilling to take any meaningful action.

Those problems were, of course, the product of a generation that simply accepted racial abuse as part of their everyday life and if you happened to be black or belong to an ethnic minority then it was something you were expected to accept without question.

For many people it was simply part of their day to day vocabulary when referring to black people and it is precisely that attitude that SRtRC has worked so hard to eradicate not just from football, but from society as a whole.

## Our message is, 'You're not born a racist, you become a racist'

# Show Racism the Red Card

# We take the

Howard Gayle, yours truly, Warren Barton & Earl Barratt

Receiving a cheque from
Hilton in the Community Foundation

In the garden of Number 10 with Prime Minister Gordon Brown - Shaka Hislop is on the right and standing next to him is the founder of 'Show Racism the Red Card', Ged Grebby

On 12th May 2008, our second Hall of Fame awards ceremony was held at 10 Downing Street and was hosted by Prime Minister Gordon Brown. The ceremony was attended by numerous high profile names from the world of sport together with celebrities from other walks of life. This photograph taken outside Number 10 includes footballers David Kelly, Dean Gordon, Howard Gayle, Brian Hall, and George Burley as well as stars from the music world, Tracey Wilkinson from Bad Girls and Heather Small, lead singer with M People.

The terrible twins,
...it's like looking in a mirror!

# Show Racism the Red Card

In July 2008 the Sunderland Former Players Association arranged a special fund-raising golf day for SRtRC, which was held at Tynemouth Golf Club. The photo left shows the 'Gary Bennett Team' and the guy on the left is my best mate Alan Stubbs. Alan is my son Andre's godfather and we've been close friends ever since we met shortly after I joined Sunderland in 1984 - in fact people call us the 'terrible twins' because wherever either of us go, you can bet the other one isn't far behind!

## MISSION STATEMENT

Show Racism The Red Card is an anti-racist educational charity. We aim to combat racism through enabling role models, who are predominantly but not exclusively footballers, to present an anti-racist message to young people and others.

Show Racism The Red Card acknowledges that racism changes, as do the experiences of Black and Minority Ethnic communities in the UK. Our message and activities therefore need to be able to respond to such changes as and when appropriate.

**We achieve this through:**
- **Producing educational resources.**
- **Developing activities to encourage people, including young people, to challenge racism.**
- **In parts of the UK, challenging racism in the game of football and other sports.**

**'Benno and I first met while he was playing for Carlisle United and I was the Carlisle commentator for BBC Radio Cumbria. Some years on I had 'transferred' to Sunderland for BBC Newcastle and was looking for a new right hand man and Benno immediately came to mind.**

He was ...is ...after all a Sunderland legend. While 'legend' is a term used often and sometimes ill-advisedly, in Benno's case it is more than justified. Wherever we go he is recognised and lauded and as often as not is asked 'what's going on Benno ...what's going on?'.

He's been as solid and reliable as my summariser as he was as a player with the endearing aberration here and there. Sunderland were at the Reebok Stadium to play Bolton and we were due on air at 2pm. At half past one Benno calls to say he's ten minutes away. 'Where are you?' I ask. 'Outside Burnden Park' he replies. 'What are you doing there ???'. He arrived at the Reebok an hour later. I never found out why he thought the Reebok Stadium was adjacent to Burnden Park.

Benno has a remarkable eye for the game. Without fail he will pre-empt substitutions and can read the game better than anyone I know. Our first match together was a pre-season friendly at Kilmarnock in August 2003 and he's barely missed a match since. At Burnley once, he and I were sitting together on the opposite side of the gangway to a Burnley fan who throughout the first half raged, ranted and railed against Sunderland's players and we felt his opprobrium feet away and at half time when he leaned across to confront us, expected a tirade of verbal abuse. He glared at us for a few seconds... "You two are the best dressed commentators I've ever seen at Burnley".

**That's Benno. Professional, immaculately turned out, always with time for the fans and great company.'**

Nick Barnes.

# A chip off the old block!

My son Andre is currently on Middlesbrough's books and I reckon he's got a decent chance of making a career in the game, although it's always difficult to predict how young players are going to develop.

**Andre surprised a few people by signing for Boro when he was more or less expected to follow in his father's footsteps and join Sunderland. To be honest it was entirely his decision and my only advice to him was to pick the club at which he felt he would be happiest.**

When Andre first went to Boro I was given the opportunity to coach the youngsters at the club's academy so over the years I've been able to keep a watchful eye on his progress. In terms of natural ability, there's no doubt he's good enough and he's certainly a much better all-round player than I was at his age - whether he can make it at the top level though, only time will tell.

...and finally, the most important thing in my life, my family.

The best move I ever made. **Marrying Audrey in Jamaica on June 17th 1991.**

Grand daughters Jasmin, Ave Marie and Katie

Step daughter Amanda

Daughter Janee and son Leon

Leon and girlfriend Vicki

Step-son Lee with wife Katrina and grandchildren Dylan, Reece and Melissa

# T.E.A.M.
## Together Everyone Achieves More

'One of the most important things I learnt as a
professional footballer was the importance of teamwork.

Individual ability is fine, but success in football can
only be achieved with the help of your colleagues and
I am indebted to the countless numbers of people who
have helped me during my career.

They taught me the most valuable lesson of all.

Together everyone achieves more!'

**Looking back on my career
in football, nothing has given me
a greater sense of achievement
than the success of our
fight against racism.**